GRADUATION

Making a Life after Teaching

Audrianne Hill

Audrianne Hill

Copyright © 2013 by Audrianne Hill
All rights reserved
Published in the United States of America

ISBN: 9781493715534

Cover and author photos by
Cheri Smith Photography

Editing, design and publishing arrangements by
Sara Leeland Books   www.saraleelandbooks.net

GRADUATION:

Making a Life after Teaching

The Next Step

Columbus was wrong. The world *is* flat,
its edges sharp and abrupt,
or at least that is how it can feel
when who we are is about to change.
Everything we knew about ourselves,
Everything we felt secure in the knowledge of
fails to hold true. The jump we are about to take
seems dangerous; the tethers seem weak.
The first step can take our breath,
but we leap anyway.
To back away from the edge would risk
the name "coward" being thrust in our direction,
would risk our admitting maybe we aren't as tough
as we told everyone we were.
Maybe we aren't ready
and what courage it takes to admit that!
All we can do is move forward,
move our toes to the edge and peer over,
looking at what adventures lie ahead.
In increments as small as a baby's crawl
or as large as a giant's lope through the bean
    patch,
we must move onward. It is time.

June 1, 2001

Table of Contents

The Next Step	v
Introduction	1
June, July and August	5
September	14
October	23
November	38
December	46
January	57
Ferbruary	89
March	95
April	107
May	120
June	145
Afterword	154
Acknowledgements	156
About the author	157

INTRODUCTION

If anyone would have told me at the age of 26, when I began my teaching career at Grand Haven Area Public Schools, that I would retire when I was 52, I would have given them a doubtful look. I must admit that 52 is still a tad too young to say one is 'retired'. Nevertheless it is true.

The ability to have such a choice I owe to my mother, herself a teacher. Following my being hired, she gave me one valuable piece of advice: "buy five years." I could not imagine needing the option to be able to retire early back in 1986, but being a dutiful daughter, I listened, buying the additional five years of social security at my first year's salary of $14,000.00. Now I'm glad I listened to mom.

Once upon a time, being an educator was a highly respected profession. Society praised teachers, parents listened to their advice—knowing the concern for their child's well-being was the intent behind giving it—and one was proud to be a member of the profession. I often said, with pride, that I was a teacher.

But by June of 2012 I found myself saying the proclamation under my breath, fearful of the verbal abuse I might receive about increased graduation standards, union power, poor test scores, and more.

The school district in which I taught hired caring and involved teachers. The awards for academics as well as athletics attest to the leadership of the staff.

Yes, there were some teachers who needed to retire and—with the additional technological skills faculty was now required to have to aid student achievement—some did let go.

One of the better decisions by the State of Michigan was eliminating the permanent teaching certificate that had allowed teachers to remain static in their skills and in their approach to the classroom. Requiring teachers to return to the classroom and earn 6 additional credits towards a higher degree enforced the grasp of new teaching methods and ideas. Nothing makes classroom management harder than a teacher who cannot engage with their students due to a lack of new information or failure to show passion for their subject.

Unfortunately the State of Michigan and our federal government have often also led in presenting teachers, especially public educators, in a less than positive light. In recent years, it is said that much of what is wrong with the nation is the fault of the education system.

Few critics note that the funding of public education is diminished by a sizable percentage every year. If we spent as much money on education as we do on our military and prison systems, fear that the United States would no longer be a leader on the world's stage wouldn't be an issue.

My decision to retire from teaching was made before any student entered my classroom in the fall of 2011. After the second day of teacher in-service prior to the beginning of the official school year, faculty and union meetings let me see the trend now in place.

I was angry at what I heard in these meetings. Once again I would have to defend myself, my teaching methods and the curriculum to a state government that refused to include classroom teachers in the decision-making process. By the following school year, we were warned, there would be a loss of personal income and an increase in health insurance costs.

Overall, staying in the career I loved was becoming more problematic than the unknowns of retirement. I decided this year would be my last. I would teach my final year and go out proud of the lessons taught, proud of the students I was honored to have in my classes, and proud of the war wounds I earned.

After the funeral of a man who died early in his 70s, Mrs. Sundberg, a resident of Garrison Keillor's Lake Wobegon, remarked that "He really didn't die with much to show for his life. I don't know that he really made a difference."

Well, she thought, "Hmm. It sounded a bit harsh, but truth is that way, and it is a bit sad to think of leaving the world one day without having been an expert in something, without having left a mark of some sort..."

I'm no expert but I know I have left a mark; I just don't know where, with whom or how deep the scar.

My years of teaching at Grand Haven High School were the most unexpected pleasure; I didn't intend to be a teacher, running away from the family profession and then stumbling into it. Having had some good teachers as examples didn't hurt. But now a leap of faith was needed.

Elizabeth Kubler Ross wrote, "How do geese know when to fly to the sun? Who tells them the seasons? How do we, humans, know when it is time to move on? As with the migrant birds, so surely with us, there is a voice within, if only we would listen to it, that tells us so certainly when to go forth into the unknown".

I am listening to that voice.

June, July and August 2012

Summer began like every other summer, but somehow I couldn't shake the notion that this summer would be different. I wouldn't be going back to the classroom in the fall. This was emphasized by all of the retirement parties—seven! Either friends and co-workers were thrilled to see me go or they were supportive of this decision to take the next leap of faith. I assumed the latter. But by the last week of June, I was having school dreams and when I would get up in the morning wonder, "What's that all about?"

I jumped right into summer, leaving for Chimney Corners in Frankfort, Michigan the day after I walked out of my classroom. Another Heneveld reunion was on the books. They have been taking place along the shores of Platte River biannually since 1951 when my maternal great-grandmother, Anna Heneveld, passed away and her twelve children, spread out across the United States, feared they would lose touch. The Frankfort area of Northern Michigan was the chosen spot as Great Uncle Louis Spencer was a captain at Point Betsie lighthouse and for many years, while my grandmother was growing up, he could procure enough cottages for the entire family to come and vacation.

Great-great Uncle Lou was a widower with two young sons. He married my great grandmother's sister, Augusta, after a few years of her employment with him as a nursemaid for the boys. The twelve Heneveld brothers and sisters with their spouses and children would arrive for an entire week of climbing Sleeping Bear Dunes, evening family picnics, paddling the Platte River to its mouth at Lake Michigan, big lake fishing as well as some smaller lake fishing, and catching up on family news. In addition to these reunions, the children of George and Anna sent a Round Robin throughout the clan. A Round Robin is a packet of letters sent from the oldest child in birth order to the youngest. As the packet reaches the next sibling, the last letter written by that sibling is replaced by a current one, the rest are read and then sent on.

  The reunions have not been as large as in previous years, as the only sibling remaining from the original twelve is 90 year-old Aunt Barb, but they're fun just the same. We still stay the entire week, try to do as many of the ritualistic activities as possible and gather every night, as we always did, for a family meal. Two of my nieces joined me this year. One arrived with her family at the beginning of the reunion and the other joined me mid-week. Grand-nephews Josiah and Isaac swam in Platte River, found turtles and caterpillars, who traumatically found themselves in the driver's seat of toy Mini Coopers.

  This year I rented a small one-bedroom cottage at Chimney Corners Resort known as Hillside, appropriately titled I think. It has a large wrap around deck looking out over M-22 towards Crystal Lake, which, when I was a child, was known as the clearest lake in the United States.

Unloading the back of my Subaru Forrester, aptly named Tucker after the actor Forest Tucker from the television series "F-Troop," I enter the main room of the cottage. To my left is a small table with seating for four. Behind it, against the north wall, is the main kitchen area. There is a small window over the kitchen sink looking out at the dune into which the cottage is built. At eye level grow brightly colored wildflowers.

Straight into the room is the sitting area—a couch and a very comfortable rocker/lounge chair. To the right of the furniture, a picture window opens out to the deck with a view of the lake across the road. What a way to greet each summer morning!

The bedroom is entered by going straight from the cottage entryway to the east. There I'll sleep on a full sized bed. The bathroom is newly renovated and it too has a little window over the sink that looks out to the dune with little flowers. Two smaller windows offer enough space for a summer breeze to swim over the bed at night, providing a good night's sleep.

The deck of my rented cottage got plenty of use—reading, entertaining, and general greeting and closing of each day. My friend, Gloria, joined me for my final night "up north" and we had a delightful time without the hassles of school inserting itself into our conversations. We ate light, drank good wine, laughed, enjoyed the Crystal Lake breezes, walked along M-22 and imagined living in the various houses that had grown up along the shoreline. But alas, I had to come home to the beginning of a heat wave.

A few years ago I constructed a brick patio in my back yard with the assistance of a neighbor. The fact I performed such grunt work amazed me, I didn't think I had it in my constitution, but, when encouraged, it is surprising what one can do. Last year I began holding monthly summer patio parties on the first Friday of the month.

I borrowed the idea from one of my aunts. Recently widowed and having moved into a new neighborhood, she walked around Grant Ave. and invited her neighbors to come over for cocktails as a way for them to get to meet and get to know her two teenage sons. I saw the patio party as a way to connect at least once a month with my neighbors other than a "Hi, how are you?" that usually doesn't elicit an honest answer to the question.

It is a nice way to begin the weekend. A little wine, a little nosh...all good. June's patio party was the Friday before school let out for the summer but a torrential downpour canceled it. Who knew that by July the next patio party would be canceled due to the heat! There wasn't an umbrella big enough to provide enough shade or a breeze strong enough to ease the humidity.

The August 2012 heat wave found me discovering a TV program I didn't have time to watch when it originally showed: *The West Wing.* It's good television and made me wish Josiah Bartlett was really President of the United States.   So far, I've not found another television show creating that kind of addiction. But in the last months of the 2011-12 school year, one of my students mentioned *Gilmore Girls* in relation to an episode involving Edgar Allen Poe, whose work we had just been studying. The student brought in the show, season by season and eventually quite a collection of students joined us for this fast-paced verbal assault of a sit-com during the lunch hour.

The school year ended at Season 6 of *Gilmore Girls*, so naturally, when I came home from the reunion I had to take Season 7 out from the local library and finish off the show. It helped pass the time hiding from the summer heat.

* * * *

The city of Holland has a fabulous farmer's market which is open twice a week, Wednesday and Saturday. During the summer I greet these mornings bright and early as I head down to the civic center and check out what is in season. The season of fruits and vegetables begins with rhubarb and asparagus, moves to the addition of strawberries, then blueberries, followed by peaches, plums, apricots, sweet corn, tomatoes, and finally the winter crops of squashes, apples and brussels sprouts.

I experienced my first free-range chicken eggs at the market and have become a convert. There is so much to look at and to buy from these local farmers I find I rarely go to the grocery store in the summer months. For the months of May through November, I become a Catholic and the Wednesday and Saturday markets are my weekly masses.

Farmers deserve respect and, unfortunately, they often get short shrift. This summer one farm had to decide what crops to save with irrigation and what others to let die as week after week there was no rain. John McCutcheon, a folk singer from the Atlanta Georgia area, sings a song that says the farmer is the man who does all the work but it is the middle man who gets most of the profit. I hope my small purchases each week encourage these Michigan farmers to hold tight and continue to sally forth to local markets.

An additional treat at the farmer's market is the food wagons. One of our local restaurants, deBoer Bakery, has a food wagon at the market every Wednesday and Saturday. As I arrive early in the morning, I enjoy one of the best cranberry almond scones I have ever eaten. Much like my days as a waitress while in college, when I got to know my customers and their "usuals." deBoer's vendor, Jared, caught on to my order very quickly. There were mornings he would see me head up the walk and call out, "We didn't get make any scones today. How about a pig in the blanket?" He knew my order but he also had backup.

* * * *

Holland also boasts one of the best summer theaters along the lakeshore. Hope Summer Repertory Theater (HSRT) has been a part of my summer days and nights since I started teaching at GHHS. One of the first friends I made during my first year was Deb, who also drove up the lakeshore from Holland. Her sister-in-law was the producing director of HSRT, which made its home on the campus of Hope College each summer. When Deb heard I was looking for summer work, she put me in touch with Mary and for the following nine summers I worked at HSRT as their Public Relations Director.

The position was fun and exciting but each year I had to juggle my two jobs for a number of weeks as the school year was ending and the summer theater just beginning. The first months of theater work involved obtaining advertisers for the program and writing up the biographies of the entire company for their publication in the program. Once school ended, there was more breathing room to meet deadlines, but it still required focus as each repertory show opened within two weeks of the previous event. By the middle of July all five of the plays were in production; a different play each night.

I continued to see a matinee and a few evening performances this summer. Mary, after close to 40 years of association with the theater was retiring at the end of the season. Her retirement party alone was a theatrical event. Think of it! So many actresses and actors who got their start at HSRT showed up one weekend for a surprise gathering. I have made some dear friends from this experience. It was wonderful to reconnect with folks who were still on the stage, had made it into television, or were now teaching at colleges and universities across the country.

****

The unbearable heat continued to hold Michigan in its furnace-like grasp through July and into August. Even Tess found going for any walk other than our early morning one too hot to handle. She would stand on the back step of the porch and give me such a look, "Seriously? You're seriously expecting me, in *this* fur coat, to come out here?" So day in and day out we hid inside as if it were a winter storm and I read—twenty books in all from June to August.

Finally a break—the temperature dropped down to 80. Who knew one could be so excited about 80 degrees? What to do but celebrate! Julia Child would have been 100 years old on August 15, so my neighbor Cheri and I plan a birthday party. We make Child's famous beef bourguignon, drink wonderful wine, and watch *Julia and Julia*, in addition to some PBS episodes of her *French Chef*. Some of Cheri's friends from Ann Arbor are in town and 17 year-old Alex is in a newly discovered state of euphoria. He had never heard of Child nor experienced such a dinner.

****

As with most open roads such as the retirement road I am on, there are dreams for what lies along their sides. The first dream is to try to do things at a slower pace. Being a professed anal-retentive person, I live by lists to make sure I "get things done." I am hoping to break a portion of that habit.

One of the first things I grew excited about when I made the decision to retire was the prospect of going out to Crane's Orchards in Fennville during the autumn season to pick apples whenever I wanted to, but now, due to the crazy spring weather we had here in Michigan, there aren't any apples to pick. One of my favorite activities of autumn, must be set aside, at least for this year. (Heavy sigh.) The farmer's market stays open until mid-December and that will have to suffice. On a positive note, when September rolls around, I will still be able to go on Wednesdays, a day I would normally be in the classroom.

There is also the dream of going East. I have been to New England many times to walk the Freedom Trail in Boston, whale watch off of Cape Ann, pretend to be a pilgrim in Plymouth and a witch in Salem, hang out with transcendentalists in Concord, pay homage to Norman Rockwell in Stockbridge and see how the Lincoln Memorial was designed in Chesterfield, the home of sculptor Daniel Chester French. But all of these trips took place over summer months or spring vacations, and I have always wanted to experience a New England autumn. Year after year, I have saved the September/October issues of *Yankee* magazine to whet my appetite for the experience. One article is about a New Hampshire town that places hundreds of carved pumpkins in the hills on October 30 and 31st. What an experience it would be to see that!

September

For many educators the New Year does not begin in January but in September, with the start of the new school year, new students and perhaps even a new curriculum.

As the State and the nation make attempts to restructure the education system, holding America's children up to the light against the children of other countries, this new year can be met with excitement but often is met with dread. Those who make the changes to be implemented in the classroom have rarely been at the head of one, and have no idea how these standards and benchmarks will be met although it certainly looks good on paper. After years of seeing the wheel reinvented or simply renamed, along with finding my pension and health insurance benefits threatened, I felt left with no alternative but to turn in my Expo markers (the chalk and its dust a mere memory) and turn out the lights one last time in June.

Even when the Back-to-School ads began to run in the newspapers and television in July, I didn't flinch. I don't think my retirement had completely sunk in. Although I spent the summer *not* putting articles, books, props, and notes for new approaches to the curriculum in the bag that traveled to and from school, I didn't feel "retired." That word meant "old," and I didn't feel that either.

Some neighbors expressed genuine concern about my next move. They rarely saw me as someone who sat still, except on a sunny day with a good book on the front porch, and they asked with serious inquiry about when, or if, I might feel the bottom drop out from beneath myself. Perhaps my going out each week and pulling the garbage containers back from the curb once the truck went by was a red flag. From my perspective I had time and it was some exercise. I mean, wouldn't you like to arrive home from a hard day at work to find bringing in the trash container one last thing you didn't have to do? I could sense their concern about all my "free time" and I assured them they wouldn't find their lawns mowed or houses painted.

I am a teacher. I always introduce myself as a teacher. What will happen when that part of my identity is no longer there? The late poet, Wislawa Szymborska, stated "Every beginning, after all, is nothing but a sequel, and the book of events is always open in the middle." I am turning a page.

My friend, Deborah, also a former teacher, came by my house one morning after dropping her grandson off at the school around the corner. She had heard Windmill Island Gardens, a local tourist attraction, needed some tour guides for the remaining eight weeks of the season. The college students had all returned to their dorms and "Wouldn't it be fun?"

Windmill Island is a small island in the middle of Black River. It was owned by a farmer, Henry Koop, who, when he passed away in 1947 bequeathed his land to the City of Holland. Some of the city's notables came up with the idea to make contacts in the Netherlands to see if Holland could purchase an actual functioning windmill. It took many years for the deal to be struck (a war got in the way), but after fifteen years the deal had been finalized and the deZwaan windmill, built in 1671, made its way across the ocean to Holland, Michigan. It was the last windmill to ever leave the country. There are now less than 90 functioning windmills in the Netherlands, the rest being left to ruin, turned into B and B's, or managed as national landmarks.

The mill arrived in pieces in the fall of 1963. It took six months for it to be reconstructed on the island and it was rededicated in April of 1964. Again the notables of the city and Prince Bernard of the Netherlands were there to mark the occasion. I was there too, but I don't remember much. I was three. My Aunt Diane was a junior at Holland High School and a member of the exhibition Dutch dance group sent out to dance at just such events throughout the year. The city asked each member provide a "mini-me," dressed in identical provincial attire, to stand with them in front of each of the Netherland provincial flags. I got my picture on the cover of *Parade* magazine, so there is proof, but I remember nothing.

The day is sunny and warm when Deb picks me up to drive out to the island. We cross the bridge and walk the property to the mill and around the farmland. We climb up the steps to the fourth floor of the mill and walk outside on the gallery where one is up close and personal to the De Zwaan's blades. Looking to the south I see across the marshy shore to the cityscape of Holland; to the north, trees just begging for cooler climes to turn color; east to the fields once tilled by Mr. Koop, and west to a watery expanse I know will take me out to Lake Michigan should I choose to find a canoe and follow it. We meet some of the other guides dressed in their Dutch garb, listen to the 1927 Amsterdam street organ and check out the 1929 carousel. The gardens are in full summer bloom, the tulips long gone from their early April arrival. The beauty of the day made it all enticing. Even the requirement of wearing a Dutch costume didn't faze me, although it should have been a warning sign.

I have long been an opponent of school uniforms, and being asked to wear t-shirts for any event the school promoted found the shirt tacked to the bulletin board rather than on my back. In this regard, I was *not* a team player. The one way a student can show their identity is through their wardrobe, as long as it isn't vulgar and inappropriate for the classroom. While some may argue restricting vulgar or inappropriate attire is a limiting of a student's identity, instruction of appropriateness of dress provides for a teachable moment. Teachers wearing t-shirts encourages them to "dress down"; it's difficult to be treated as a professional when one fails to dress as one.

My job as a tour guide provided an hourly wage to off-set my pension deductions for taxes and health insurance. More importantly it gave me an opportunity to be outside, and talk to people without a paper to grade, a phone call home, or a late night of Parent-Teacher conferences. All I had to do is "be nice." Still, I can't help inserting the story behind *The Crucible* when I take my tour to the second floor of the windmill. The second floor is the packaging floor where the organic flour ground by the mill is bagged in two or three pound bags.

As a guide I am instructed to tell tourists that, should they purchase some of the flour from the gift shop, it needs to be stored in the refrigerator or freezer as it can spoil quicker due to a lack of preservatives. This factor provided one theory about what caused the hysteria of the girls of Salem that ,ade them cry out "witch" and send eighteen individuals to their deaths. That fact has nothing to do with the actual tour but I can't help myself. As I make the connection to this historical event I want to share my "discovery" with others. Once a teacher, always a teacher.

One afternoon while up on the fourth floor gallery with a tour group, a flock of Canadian geese flew by at our eye level. It was breathtaking to be so close to these birds. It made that day, and in my own mind made the job worth it. But, as the eight weeks passed, so did my initial enthusiasm. It isn't the tourists, the staff, the hours, the tour script, it's the costume. My provincial attire was a man's Strophorst. If I were truly male and truly from Strophorst, my attire would tell the world I was a farmer. It was a simple blue shirt, red kerchief, black pants and cap, and wooden shoes that curved in each tip to denote me a farmer rather than a fisherman. A fisherman's wooden shoe would have a more pointed end so they could use the point to hook the nets.

My animosity toward the uniform begins to rear its ugly head as each morning I look to my closet full of clothes I wore to the classroom, and then have to reach for pants, shirt, kerchief and shoes. My first real pangs of missing school is not missing students or discussing the curriculum, Puritanism, which is September's unit, but my inability to dress the part of a tour guide.

I also realize my commitment to this job means no trip to "leaf peep" in New England. I experience a bit of regret but tell myself I do not have to do everything on my list following retirement in the first year. Perhaps a trip north to the Benzie and Leelanau counties will suffice. I am queen of delayed gratification.

* * * *

When I left the high school in June amidst hugs and moans from my sophomores and hugs and deer-in-the-headlight looks from my seniors who were also on the threshold of change, I hadn't looked much beyond the idea of not having to set my alarm clock for 4:30 AM. I allow my collie, Tess, to determine my wake-up call. It's 6:00 AM. I also looked forward to sitting on my front porch in the morning, slowly drinking cup after, if desired, cup of coffee reading the morning paper.

This I do, but I feel a bit sheepish about it. As each neighbor pulls out of their drive, I feel a tug to duck down and not be seen. While I am basking in the glow of this wonderful freedom, I don't want to flaunt it. Having the opportunity to do what I want when I want goes against something I managed to have seep into my soul from all that Puritanism put forth in Arthur Miller's play.

Life stopped being a list of things to do because my plate was full and my obsessive-compulsive side had to make sure things got done. Instead, I now have a list of things to do because I have the time to forget to do them and they eventually *need* to get done. I let go of my sense of accountability and reconfigured my daily tasks. On days when I am scheduled to work at the island, nothing else gets done until I get home, On days when I am not scheduled to work, however, the hours can easily slip by minute by minute as I simply stare out into space, my space of my own choosing.

* * * *

Fall is my favorite season. I look forward to September 23 with as much childhood anticipation as Halloween and Christmas. By Labor Day weekend the first pumpkins begin to make their way into the stalls at the farmer's market. Actual fall decorations have been on Hobby Lobby and Michaels store shelves for at least a month but I refrain.

Still, Labor Day! September! Pumpkins! I feel like Linus in *It's The Great Pumpkin, Charlie Brown* as he spies that newly raked pile of leaves. Geronimo! I want to jump right into the pumpkin spirit. I do give in and buy a variety of pumpkins to decorate the front steps but hold off until the 23rd for my annual fall onslaught of decorating. I have never asked my postal worker how he/she feels about having to maneuver the mail to my front door mail slot, but my neighbor, Bob, walks by and looking my way mutters, "Damn pumpkins," with a smile that encourages me to put out a few more.

To curb my anticipation and excitement about decorating, I get into Fall Fairy mode and wrap fall presents for friends. This year Gloria gets a basket of apples and leaves to decorate her door; Vonnie receives a scented candle; Angela, a small banner to don her condo walkway; Mark and Mick in Chicago are sent russet colored candles for entertaining, and others receive autumn scented hand soaps—Creamy Pumpkin, Orchard Walk, Apple Cider, Sweet Cinnamon Pumpkin. With autumn's arrival on Saturday I need to get into fairy flight on Friday so as not to be detected.

The 23rd is also the 15th Susan G. Koman Race for the Cure which my family runs/walks in memory of my mother who passed away from breast cancer on August 8, 2005. Mailing the candles requires sending the package out by the 17th. For the rest, it is Operation Friday Fairy Flight.

The Susan G. Koman Race for the Cure requires me to leave the house by 7:30 to get to the meeting spot at the mall in Grandville. My niece, Misti, began to participate in this race the year of my mother's death. Mom was five and a half years into her remission from cancer when it returned. I thought we were out of the woods and I couldn't bring myself to participate the first year after her death. I was busy dealing with my father's grief, failing to grieve myself as I plunged into the school year. But the following year, I felt I needed to participate to honor my mother. My goal is to walk the race in an hour or less. I manage with three minutes to spare.

      I arrive home from the morning race in time to listen to NPR's "Wait, Wait, Don't Tell Me," which to one of my friends is known as "Wait, Wait, Don't Call Me." I refuse to answer the phone for the hour. As Peter Sagal is quizzing his panel about the week's news, I am heading up and down the steps to the basement where the Rubbermaid tubs lie full of pumpkins. There are glass ones, ceramic ones, naturally dried ones, cloth ones, and they all find their home on my Stickney buffet in the dining area. Banners welcoming the season get hung from the house and grace the yard walk, stackable pumpkins in urns sit by the garage and front walk, more pumpkins glow from their stands on the front porch, along with an urned pumpkin emblazoned with "Icabod" and a tri-corner hat to greet whoever comes to the door. Various nooks and crannies find themselves filled with leaves, small- er pumpkins, acorns, and crows. By the end of the day I am pleasantly and glowingly exhausted. I can't wipe the smile from my face no matter how hard I try

October

The days at Windmill Island are nearing their end. Autumn's signature has arrived with a burst of maple leaf and aspen along the roadsides as the last of summer's heat begs to hang on for just one more day.

There are pumpkins lined up in neat little rows at a farm on Holland's Graafschap Road. Each row bears a sign with the price for the squashes of comparable size. I have quite a few pumpkins at home already but I can't help myself and find three different sizes which I can stack and place in one last urn. I choose a bright Cinderella pumpkin for the base, topped with a Blue Globe and finally a mottled yellow one whose name I do not know but like for its adding diversity to the others.

Little towns dotting the shores of Lake Michigan are now decorated in their finest autumn splendor. There are hay bales, and scarecrows and witches tied like Odysseus to the mast of his ship, but here adorning lamp posts. Leaf tendrils drop down to greet these figures, as arts and crafts fairs dot local parks. For a short time, anyone traveling through is a member of these villages, joining in the fun and frivolity.

* * * *

Holland's Hope College had become the next educational step for a few of my 2012 seniors. In June I'd given my email address to my seniors with the stipulation: no butt dialing. ('Butt dialing' happens when a phone is placed in ones back pocket and a number is dialed when the person sits down—I've gotten a few of these calls at 2 in the morning.) I told them they were ready for this next adventure but sometimes we all need someone to hold our hand and tell us we're okay. I'd be honored and happy to help them make this transition.

If 'help!' meant assistance with writing, the only guideline was to allow me enough time between when a paper would be due and when they would like me to take a look at it. Previously a former student studying at Lake Superior State College sent a paper to me asking for a check—but he needed it back in two hours. Sadly, I couldn't fulfill that wish. I was still teaching and didn't have my planning period until after his deadline.

In September I received some initial contacts. "Hey, Ms. Hill, I'm here at Hope and just thought I would check in. I like Hope. I like Holland. I like my professors...." By the beginning of October, with their semester fully underway, I began to get editorial inquiries. Will and Ethan, who were roommates, asked if I would have time to edit their papers in the way we had done in our College English class. Julia wrote to tell me she was enjoying running for the cross country team and was writing a paper on ALS. She wanted to thank me for introducing her to Morrie Schwartz from Mitch Albom's book, *Tuesdays With Morrie*, which we studied for the authentic living unit in humanities class. She was planning to include portions of it in her paper.

It felt good to put the editor hat back on, if only for these brief moments. It was also great to reunite with these young people who were doing just fine in the world of college academia.

I also received an email from Tracy, my former principal, asking for retired teachers to come in and help students with their essays for college applications. This was part of a week-long activity geared toward getting as many seniors as possible applying to colleges. I had read many such essays for former students in the past and I liked this idea. The previous year we had tried this activity in the spring, targeting juniors, but it didn't work out so well. Juniors weren't focused on applications yet and we got little participation. Fall seemed a perfect time to jump-start their final year in high school and position them for a collegiate career.

I thought my first time back at school would give me a weird feeling, but that didn't happen. I had no hesitation walking into the school as a former teacher. The large conference room off the main office was set aside for this activity and there were at least seven other retired teachers already in the room. More than half were former English teachers.

Sadly, the hour we were asked to be there for students turned into a reunion instead of a work session. Only one student arrived for help with his essay. The most recent pair of retired teachers had been out of the school system for five years, so the student felt more comfortable getting assistance from me.

Shortly after he left, word got out I was in the building and as the other teachers were catching up on each other's lives, I found myself out in the main hallway of the building receiving and giving hugs to former students.

It felt good to be missed. Students eyes grew wide with my presence and even Krystal, wheeling up in her chair, shouted out a greeting prior to my bending down to give her a hug. There was no "What are you doing here?" It seemed they didn't care what brought me to school, what mattered is that I was there. Many were on their way to the cafeteria so time was short. I asked who their English teacher was this year and assured them they were in a good class. It became quite comical as, instead of helping with essays, I was giving out hugs!

* * * *

Halloween decorations begin to creep out of storage from their Rubbermaid tubs in the basement. Little papier-mâché trick-or-treaters made by Lori Mitchell joined the pumpkins on the buffet.

These decorations reminded me of a simpler time in my childhood when parents didn't need to instill fear in their children. Don't misunderstand. There are plenty of reasons for being cautious. This age of technology forces us to teach our children to be careful and vigilant, and it doesn't end when they go off to college. Even I became an occasional 'parent' in the classroom reminding my students that what they put out on the internet stays there and they cannot erase it. It will follow them well beyond their college lives and into the work force.

Today, the former Halloween events in elementary school are either renamed Harvest Festivals or being canceled altogether. Some schools schedule professional development days for teachers instead of facing the possibility of irate parents calling about the issue of 'pagan celebrations'. Are we really so fearful of witches, ghosts, action figures, and yes, zombies that we need to take the fun out of school? Spending one day having fun will not lower any MEAP score, trust me.

There are still a few elementary schools that allow the costumes and the parade through the classrooms. I love that! In the North Muskegon Elementary School, the kindergarten class lines up and begins the parade through the first grade classroom. As they head out of the room, the first grade lines up behind and they parade through the second grade and on through each classroom, then they walk out into the neighborhood on the sidewalk along the path leading to the local library. This year, because of inclement weather, they have to parade to the gymnasium where, standing in a large circle against the walls, everyone can view the vast array of ghosts and goblins. Yes, I said, "ghost." BOO!

We are taking away innocence and forcing our children to grow up too soon. By the age of 6, our girls are dressing like Brittney Spears. Many kids have cell phones by age 10. Historically children have often been treated like little adults, but the type of adult created by the current media is one not worth emulating. Sadly, many people cannot see how much of their soul they are selling when they buy into 'what is in fashion'. We need to take back our souls.

* * * *

These last warm days, and the end of the tourist season at Windmill Island, allow me time for yard work. October 2012 in Michigan went down in the record books as the seventh wettest, but I still managed to rake the leaves (hesitant to drop any earlier than they have to) and to wrap in burlap the Japanese maple that lives at the edge of my house. I put the patio furniture in the basement, managing one more patio party on the first Friday in October.

My 6:00 AM walk through the neighborhood park is still dark, since daylight savings time will not take effect until the end of the month. Tess and I walk daily, most often not meeting any other dogs and their persons. But on occasion there are other shadows that cause her to stop and ponder before moving forward in her morning check of pee-mail.

There are many mornings I note things normally missed when we used to take this walk at 4:30 AM before I headed off to school. Now we meet the neighbor one street over as he waits in his driveway for his ride to work. He always gives Tess a pat on the head and then asks, "How's Tessie this morning?" We exchange niceties and continue on our way. It will be interesting to see the changes in the neighborhood once snow comes. In previous years I felt as if Tess and I owned the streets as we were the first ones to cross unmarked snow. Who will have that honor this year?

* * * *

Each month when my church newsletter arrived in the mail I used to experience a bit of jealousy as I read what book the church book club was reading. I was the kid on the outside of the group and I longed to be a part of it—it looked so cool. But the club met in the afternoon when I was still north in Grand Haven, teaching my final hour of the day.

The books they discussed were current and topical, not necessarily part of the western canon. Joining the club was one of the first things I did once the church year got underway. We began by reading *Caleb's Crossing* by Geraldine Brooks, about the first Native American to graduate from Harvard. Each month a new book, a new adventure.

Classroom discussion of novels was different. I was leading the conversation and each year the direction rarely changes. It is still fun to discuss the classics and see the lights go on in student's eyes. I often read to my sophomores. I don't care if they are 15 or 16 years of age, statistics show people like to be read to.

I also know that reading aloud helped many understand the text. Today's students are not used to the language of many classics. It is important to help them any way one can, and if that means reading the entire novel, so be it.

When we read Steinbeck's *Of Mice and Men*, I would try to alter Lennie's voice so students can see his mental challenges. When reading Harper Lee's *To Kill A Mockingbird*, I would read slower with a slight southern drawl but more importantly, order them not to read it out of class. I love the book too much not to want to be a part of their "mockingbird" experience. Often a student would come up and privately say, "I know you told us not to read ahead but I couldn't help it." Then they would confess to reading the entire book. We must train good readers, they don't happen naturally. One must learn to love books by seeing others love books and catching the disease.

* * * *

Maybe it was the rainy month or the lack of heat in the windmill but during the last days of my job at the island, I caught a cold. I rarely catch colds. Two years ago I had five colds in one school year. I blame it on Capturing Kids Hearts. That year the school district instituted a program to curb negative behaviors such as absenteeism and bullying, and promote a strong student-teacher relationship in all classrooms.

I was skeptical. Capturing Kids Hearts is the brain child of Flip Flippen. Yep, that's his real name. It creates an atmosphere of ownership, trust and learning in the classroom beginning at the classroom door. This program includes all grade levels with the theory that once it is learned at the elementary level, it will be a no-brainer at the secondary levels. At the beginning of each day, or class period, the teacher is at the door greeting students with a handshake as they enter the room. For elementary teachers, this is a one-time event. For secondary educators however, this can happen five times a day. It can become very time consuming. But this is where, I believe, the common cold entered my world and decided to never leave.

I always greeted my students at the door. It was a way to monitor hall activity, greet others, in addition to my students, but also to have private one-on-ones without drawing attention in the classroom setting. The first year I agreed to play by the rules and despite my attempts to wash my hands with anti-bacterial lotion, I couldn't stop the virus. There is so much that needs to be done in the course of a class hour, each minute is precious. Once the door is closed, attendance taken, and the events of the evening discussed, I needed to get moving. Time flew.

So last year I decided to buck the system. I could not afford to be sick and be off my game. No one could teach my classes the way I could. I needed to be there. I owed it to the kids in my room. I was upfront about my civil disobedience. On the first day of classes,

I shook hands as what was expected but then I informed each class that it was both the first and the last time. I explained the five colds caught in the previous year and my theory about how cold-germs had infiltrated my body. The kids got it—and they were cool with it.

I'd still be at the door. I would fist bump them, give them side hugs, but no more passing of moisture and germs between hands. I wasn't sick the entire year. Coincidence? Nah.

With the days at the windmill over, I was ready to begin retirement. It didn't last long. On the third day I received a telephone call from Lisa, one of the owners of the downtown independent bookstore, *Readers World*. One of their employees was relocating to Connecticut, and she had heard I was "retired but fun." Might I be interested in coming to work for them?

Readers World has been my bookstore since I was old enough to go downtown by myself on a Saturday afternoon once my chores were finished. Lisa's two older brothers were a couple of years older than me, and my 1970's hormonal self found them to be incredibly cute. David Cassidy and Donny Osmond cute. I'd be dropped off on the corner of 8th Street and River Avenue in front of the store and have two hours to window shop, block after block, returning to the bookstore at the designated pick-up time. If Jeff or Chris were helping out at the store I would return a bit earlier so I could go in and peer over the aisle of books and magazines, averting my eyes if they should look up. If Ernie was working I would do serous book shopping but if one of the boys were at the register, I couldn't bring myself to buy a book.

Even now I stop by the bookstore every Sunday following church to pick up a book I have ordered from hearing it mentioned on some NPR program, or to purchase a magazine. I do have some magazine subscriptions mailed to my house but there's something special about going into the bookstore and discovering a new monthly issue of *Food and Wine* on the shelf.

Anne is my bookseller and I love the way she has learned my reading pattern. Just this month she directed me to Mary Oliver's *Ten Thousand Mornings.*

Following church I stopped in as usual and asked Anne if she had heard Lisa had called me with an invitation to come and work at the store. She had. I wondered if I could do it. It had been a long time since I had worked retail and I had never worked a cash register or a credit card machine. Anne assured me that learning those things would be a cinch and my knowledge of books would be an added bonus. I appreciated her confidence.

No sooner had I accepted the job at the bookstore than I received an email from Tracy at Grand Haven High School, asking me to call her ASAP. Holly, one of the English teachers, was going to go on medical leave in December for fused vertebrae surgery.

Tracy wanted me to come in and be Holly's long-term substitute because I already knew the curriculum. In fact, the entire curriculum was mine as I had seen Holly struggle with the American literature course when she first arrived at GHHS and had shared many of my assignments so she had room to breathe as she taught an entire new course.

On the one hand it felt so awful to have to say no to Tracy's request as I could do the assignment with no problem, but on the other hand, I had already made a verbal commitment to the bookstore and the six weeks I would be driving back up to Grand Haven would be the worst time to be driving north; it would be snowing all the time!

The worst part of my teaching year was always the weather in winter. I abhorred driving to school in bad weather. While I must give the current superintendent credit in his choice of calling snow days, there have been times when I made the drive all the way up US31, taking twice as long as normal, only to arrive at school and hear that the then-superintendent had just canceled school. Argh! So I explained my predicament and Tracy understood. Still, what a compliment to be asked to come back.

When I taught I would be caught up with feelings of angst when friends would come into town to visit. I wanted to let go and really enjoy their arrival and not care how much time I would spend with them, but instead I would be torn between wanting to give them my attention and the papers that were sitting on my dining room table at home waiting to be corrected. I demanded too much from myself; being a teacher first, I wanted to give my students twenty-four hour turnaround on the papers they turned in. Now I really think they would not have minded if it took me an extra day to correct their assignments.

So I was delighted when a mid-October weekend found me immersed with friends from New York City and Chicago, as well as the companionship of my little bedroom slipper of a canine variety grandniece, Lily.

Thom was in town from New York City visiting his mom before she headed down to Florida for the winter months. Our friendship goes back to our days at Summer Theater where I manned the public relations desk and Thom was the costume designer for the season opener, *Oliver!* I remember Thom's first instruction to cast members to "please wear underwear when you go to your costume fittings." Now living in New York City, Thom is experiencing a career change of his own—from designing for the stage to teaching and doing more philanthropic work.

He hadn't been in town for two years and it was good to sit across from him at the breakfast table and talk about our lives without the looming pile of papers waiting, like the sword of Damocles, to strike should I find myself having too much fun.

From Chicago, my friend Mark and his acting partner, David, arrived to perform one of their children's plays at the Gerald R. Ford Museum in Grand Rapids. There are never enough hours in the evening to spend with these two. Discussing plays, films, books, takes up a good portion of the evening between bites of dinner. While I see them at least twice a year when they come into the area to perform, there is still more left on the table not discussed when we need to call it a night.

Again, the fear of an early morning wake-up would be hovering in the recesses of my brain. But not this year! This year, the night was still young at 10:00 PM and it was only the guys who needed to head back to their beds that made us leave the table, napkins resting across our plates, glasses empty.

* * * *

Lily, my favorite canine, comes to visit on occasion when my niece leaves town. Unlike my aging and diva-like Tess, Lily is full of energy and an almost sickening affection. If she were a person, she would need major counseling in the area of loving to the point of stalking. It is dear to be loved so much while her family is in absentia but... If I am in the shower, she is outside the curtain on the bathmat; if I standi by any sink—bathroom or kitchen—she is directly behind me guarding the rear; the minute I sit, she becomes a lap dog.

The amount of entertainment we provide for the neighbors as we go for our walks is a lesson in humility. Imagine a Martha Graham modern dance with steady Tess providing the balance and Lily offering the nimble leaps of a young Giselle. Me, I have all I can do to keep the leashes untangled. Our walks at any time of day or night are memorable and beat any Zumba routine.

* * * *

Halloween! Candy? Check. Witch's hat? Check. Glass of red wine? Check? I'm ready to greet the Iron Men, zombies, and witches. When I moved into this neighborhood, it held an older crowd. In the 19 years since, there have been job relocations, a moved by the Hayes to assisted living, a divorce and a marriage. The new neighbors are young couples—and what do young couples do? They procreate!

Nora and Ellis arrive at my front door as Charlotte and Wilbur from *Charlotte's Web.* Arlo and Eli walk up as Luke and Yoda. Nate is a big fluffy dog who reminds me of Nana from *Peter Pan*, and Simon, Luke and little Philip are the farmer, his cow and a pumpkin. This is what Halloween is all about; making memories as they walk about the neighborhood among friends.

Growing up amid blueberry fields ten miles from town, there weren't many houses to walk up to for trick-or-treating. Mom would put us in the car and we would drive across town to go begging for candy at my Grandma Timmer's house. We knew who all of her neighbors were, and it wasn't the amount of candy collected that was important; it was being able to participate in the experience. Halloween is important for me, and knowing some of my neighbors are particular about what their children eat, I give animal crackers to some rather than chocolate bars. It's all good as far as I'm concerned.

November

November comes in a bit cloudy and, once Halloween is over, many folks have begun winterizing their homes and yards more seriously. As I'm driving, I notice more wood being stacked against garages and outbuildings, leaves raked to the curb, storm windows going up in preparation for the inevitable snow.

For me, the last tasks are to wrap the air conditioner in a tarp and my Japanese maple in burlap. I put it off because I enjoy looking at the maple so much as it lives at the corner of my house. To wrap it up is putting it to bed, and I am rarely ready to do that. Still, knowing the beautiful gift it will present to me in the spring with its red leaves is worth saying "goodbye" for a while. Delayed gratification.

The Halloween decorations and pumpkins on the buffet have been replaced by a cornucopia and antique turkey planters one would send to relatives in years past. Again, new banners go up outside the house while others come down. Fall is not over yet even though the stores have begun to display their Christmas decorations. In some stores it started even before Halloween. This is another example of how we rush through life. I like to take each holiday as it comes. We can't rush the seasons or other events in our life, so why do we rush from one holiday to the next? We need to breathe, take the day in, honoring it as it comes.

* * * *

About every eighth Sunday I am a lay leader at my church's earliest morning service. This month I lead the All Saints Day service. I love this service, more than Advent services and the Easter service which do not change in their themes. The scripture changes each year for this service but the thin veil between this world and the next does not. I am not talking about ghosts but rather the recognized connection we have to our ancestors and other loved ones who have died.

In preparation for this service I read a sermon by Barbara Brown Taylor quoting Frederick Beuchner, who noted that God drops little handkerchiefs into our lives in the manner of everyday saints—the ones who have their own faults but do good for their fellow man.

I think of all the handkerchiefs being draped over the east coast in the villages of New Jersey, New York, Connecticut in the aftermath of Hurricane Sandy, doing what they can to help—and am thankful for the handkerchiefs in my own life.

* * * *

I began my position at the bookstore mid-month. The hours allow me to still feel retired but also feel a sense of purpose. With so many books within arm's reach, I might easily owe the store more money than my paycheck puts in my pocket. In fact, I am managing a good deal of restraint, having purchased only one book since my employment.

I like the feeling of spreading the wealth of books to others. I enjoy putting a good book in the hands of a customer. I think Doris Kearns Goodwin owes me some portion of her royalties for my encouragement to customers who buy her book, *Team of Rivals,* after a conversation about the film, *Lincoln,* now showing in the local theater.

* * * *

The smell from the kitchen when a turkey is cooking is mouthwatering. It doesn't matter what I had for breakfast, once those smells begin to emanate from the oven all bets are off. My stomach wants turkey.

Benjamin Franklin wanted the turkey to be our national bird, not the bald eagle. I agree with his points about the smartness of the turkey and its beautiful plumage and also that the eagle is a more violent bird; but I would hate to think we would be prohibited from having a turkey at Thanksgiving because we would be eating our national emblem.

In my heart, the turkey will always reign supreme among birds, but I will eat it anyway.

* * * *

Following Thanksgiving, it is time to change holiday decorations. The fall decor comes down. Urns and wreaths are returned to the basement; pumpkins that could not be diced up and frozen for pastas and soups are put in the yard waste container; framed prints and turkeys go back in their Rubbermaid containers for another year.

Christmas greetings replace them. My little three-foot Christmas tree sits on the buffet and is lit by candelabra prisms recovered from a candelabra repair shop that was being torn down. My late friend, Brad, living in New York City at the time, saw the demolition of the store on his walk home one day and ran to his apartment to get any and all containers to recover as many prisms as he could.

When I put the prisms up I think of him and also my mom. I chose this tree the year she was diagnosed with breast cancer.

Next to the tree I have my crèche made from found pieces of driftwood I collected on one of my winter walks along the shores of Lake Michigan. Living along this wide expanse of water is one of life's greatest gifts and I try not to take it for granted that I have such a beautiful view just moments from my door.

I don't play Christmas music in the house until the morning following Thanksgiving. Each holiday deserves its time. But, the minute I wake, the first CD that goes on the stereo is *A Charlie Brown Christmas* by the Vince Guaraldi Trio.

That music takes me back to my youth when I waited until the holiday special would come on the television. It was always during a school night and woe to me if it was scheduled on a Wednesday night when we were expected to go to catechism. I would try so hard to convince my parents I was coming down with some mysterious illness in order to stay home.

Following the initial CD, a stack covering all ranges of the musical spectrum line up in succession to be played,

In complete juxtaposition to my fall conviction that more is more, when it comes to Christmas, less is more. At a time in our society when things can get out of control with folks displaying 6,000 lights in various manners on their homes, inflatable characters resting on their lawns—I think that something gets lost in the brilliance that blinds.

I don't really begrudge their excitement, but as the season of winter begins to envelop and quiet our walks and cushion the sounds in the street, so does my soul become quieter. The twinkle in my heart is still there but it doesn't have to beam out like some airstrip runway lighting.

* * * *

I received an email from Will, my former student, now at Hope College. He would like to see me before he heads home for the holidays following exams.

We agree to meet at the Kletz, Hope's coffee shop in the lower level of the DeWitt Center.

I arrive 20 minutes early to stop at the college's bookstore which is just down the corridor from the coffee shop. I love to go in and see what the English department is teaching. Unfortunately, the textbook section of the store is roped off. Books are arriving for the next semester and are stacked in boxes in front of the department sections' empty shelves. Bummer.

I return to the Kletz, now full of students, claiming a table near a group of serious young men. I can tell they are serious because, when I take off my coat and wrap it around the back of the chair, I overhear the word, "existentialism" from one young man's mouth and another responds, "Yes, that's it exactly." Philosophy majors? At one recent college-day event. I sat in on an introduction to philosophy lecture. The conversation I was trying not to eavesdrop on sounded much like that lecture.

In the fall, the college holds an Arts and Humanities Day, basically a college visitation day with a twist. High school students sign up to attend three hours of classes of their choice prior to arriving for the day. The classes cross all sections of the academic curriculum. As a chaperone in the past, I loved to come and sit in on classes as well. We'd arrive early so I could walk my students through the campus to alleviate fears of getting lost.

Following the morning sessions I'd take them to Van Zoeren library and give them another tour. In preparation, I had already encouraged them to use local college libraries. Grand Haven is fortunate to have two college libraries, one at Hope College and another on the Allendale campus of Grand Valley State University.

Will arrives at the Kletz with a Christmas wreath in his arms, a thank you gift for my help with his papers. I am truly touched. He bought it with his mom while home for Thanksgiving and wanted to get it to me before I bought a wreath of my own.

I don't tell him I have already purchased one that went up on my front door on Black Friday, when everyone else was out shopping. Still I am a firm believer that one can never have too many wreaths and I know exactly where this one will go—there is a section of wrought iron fencing that is just waiting for a bit of color and this is it!

I buy a cup of coffee and Will gets a Mountain Dew. "I live off this stuff," he exclaims. The Kletz crowd is beginning to thin out. We discuss a paper topic meant to provoke controversy: the exploitation of the color pink when used to raise money for breast cancer. This will be Will's final exam, and the topic could not be dearer to my heart.

Will knows my mother died from breast cancer, but he didn't know how much I abhor the color pink and the fact it drips like Pepto Bismal during the month of October. He tells me about his research and I share a recent clip that I on heard on NPR's *Here and Now*. He has a good start and asks if he can send me his draft next week, prior to turning it in? I will be looking forward to it. The teaching doesn't stop, the classroom expands.

December

My first clementine of the season; a little sun in the palm of my hand! Coming home from the grocery store I take out from the cupboard a white restaurant-ware vegetable bowl with a thin green stripe and place a mound of orange suns in it. It's a beautiful sight, a Christmas decoration all its own. Ever eat a clementine? They are so easy to peel by hand and break up into tiny little sections. A clementine is the perfect companion for travel.

I often took one or two to school each day for lunch—the apples purchased from the farmer's market stalls by then a distant memory. When I was growing up, my mom would put a navel orange in the toe of our Christmas stockings but their skin is so thick it requires a knife to cut the sections open. I saw in the grocery store ad that a navel orange is selling for $2.00 an orange. Yea for the clementine at $4.99 for a bunch!

I often ate my lunch at my classroom desk even though many magazine articles spoke out against such thing, stating one needed to break up the work space and lunch space, as well as needing to take a mental break. I wanted my students to know where they could find me should they need assistance in their assignments.

Each year when the schedule was being designed, I would ask the registrar to try to schedule my planning hour and lunch hour to cover all student lunch hours. That way there would be no reason a student could not get to me for help. If I had to leave the classroom, I would leave them a note about where I had gone and when I would be back. I firmly believed in open communication and a partnership in education. If I expected them to meet a deadline, I wanted them to know I was there to clarify, help in paper organization, and assist in the processing of ideas.

In my very last trimester my lunch hour turned into TV hour as we watched *Gilmore Girls,* seasons one through six. It was my way to connect with my students and in this day and age, it is important to connect any way one can.

* * * *

As the official Christmas shopping season begins, the bookstore hours are extended to accommodate the needs of customers. *Readers World* only had to extend its hours by one, since it stays open all year long until 8:00 PM. Customer traffic begins slowly, but as each week towards Christmas appears, it picks up.

The city of Holland begins the season with an open house in which participating stores offer discounts, cookies, hot chocolate, and a variety of fun things to bring customers in to the store. The next week the town has the Parade of Lights which requires every float, walker, truck, etc. who are in the parade line-up to be lit up in some form.

One year I walked the parade route with Tess and another couple who also had collies. We had lights strung on their leashes. I was hyped for this event, wanting to show off Tess in all her collie glory. It was a nightmare. Our little canine group was placed after a band and in front of the basket of a hot air balloon. Between the drums and the hot air balloon ejecting its flame, the dogs were a hysterical mess. Collies are a gentle breed and this was a clear assault on their psyches. Children kept running out from the sides of the route asking, "Can we pet your dog? Can we pet your dog?" and the parade route director kept yelling, "Keep your group moving!" By the third block, we stepped out of the lineup. I couldn't take it any longer, nor could Tess.

Another holiday event, scheduled by the Downtown Merchants Association, is Shopping Jam in which the stores open very early and staff are dressed in their pajamas. Specials are offered to folks who come in and shop in their jammies too. The bookstore offered coffee and donuts—but the art gallery down the street was offering pancakes! Needless to say, the line in front of the art gallery was out its door.

One night an older gentleman came into the store looking a bit bewildered. I asked if I could help him. He said he was looking for a book by a woman who cooks in her bare feet. His wife watches the show on television all of the time. Smiling, I said he was talking about the Barefoot Contessa. "Yes, and she has some foolproof book out!" he exclaimed.

We walked over to the cookbook section and I pulled the book from the shelf. He took it, began thumbing through the pages, and asked, "Is this dumb? I have been married to this woman for over fifty years."

"It's not an appliance," I said. Then I added that by purchasing this book he was showing that he was paying attention to her interests. If he really wanted to impress her, I suggested he look through the book prior to wrapping it and put a post-it note on pages that had recipes he might like her to try. "Oh, you're good," he said. Another customer satisfied.

* * * *

It is the winter solstice, the longest night of the year. For the people of Newtown, Connecticut (site of a school shooting tragedy), I am sure this past week has been never-ending. It will take much longer for them to heal and try to make sense of the slaughter, by a very ill young man, of almost an entire first grade class of students. As the friend of someone whose mentally-ill son took his life in 1992, I feel especially guarded in responding to the acts committed by those labeled mentally ill.

The hardest thing for me was to hear the news media use the consistent number—26—as if the mother, who was the first victim, and the shooter himself didn't matter.

There were 28 victims on December 14. The young man was a victim of a society who failed to help him, and his mother was a victim who had sought help for her son but came up against walls. We cannot ignore the fact that our society has let many who suffer from mental illness fall through the cracks of health care, knowing that parents or caregivers can only do so much on their own. I am not diminishing the murder of 26 teachers, administrators and first graders; I am only saying the story does not end there.

My immediate response was to drive up to my high school. I needed to be with my school family.

I easily remember the morning of September 11, 2001. It was first hour, my humanities class. Shortly after 9:00 AM, the fire alarm went off. It was not scheduled as a drill, and turned out to triggered by an art room kiln. As we walked out of the building, Joanie, who taught in the room next to mine, said her husband would never fly again. She had had CNN on her TV and they said a plane had flown into one of the Twin Towers in New York.

I didn't think much of it, but when we returned to the room and as students were finding their seats, I turned on CNN just in time to see the second plane hit. I left my room, walked to Joanie's and said, "It wasn't an accident. We're being attacked."

History was being made with the world watching. I remembered walking down the main hall when I heard the space shuttle blew up. Those "where were you when" moments are happening much too often.

* * * *

Since I no longer have to leave home at six in the morning to avoid heavy traffic on the highway and have a quiet classroom for forty minutes, I have the opportunity to participate in an activity I have long admired others for—the ability to work the crossword puzzle from the morning newspaper.

Once the newspaper articles about events of the day have been perused, editorials read and internally argued, and obituaries noted, I pull the cartoon section from the paper, fold it in quarters and begin to respond to the hints posted for the game of crossword.

I don't have a set pattern for attacking the puzzle. I know there are people who read all of the 'Across' hints first and then go on to the 'Down' hints. I start at '1-Across' but I often find I am searching the entire puzzle for ones I know are sure bets. An entire section fills in quite easily once two or three words are found in a particular corner.

The puzzle gets harder as the week extends. By Friday the puzzle can be found on the kitchen counter for the length of a day, while I consider it each time I pass through. Sometimes it takes time away from it to see obvious answers.

When I finish the puzzle I feel as if one of my elementary teachers just came down the row and placed an assignment back on my desk with the letter A in the top right hand corner. Something so simple brings such childish pleasure.

* * * *

The week before Christmas is busy at the bookstore, but the evenings slow down after 8:00 PM. Customers come in looking for something—some having exact titles, others with an author, and still others with the idea of what the book is about so that a guessing game ensues. For the most part customers leave satisfied with their purchases. As Christmas gets closer, however, a desperate tone appears in the voices of many. They want a best-seller, when our last copy just went out the door in the bag of the previous customer. They are disappointed and I endure the glare.

The bookstore is small. It can't hold the number of books a big box bookstore can. Nor does it offer CDs. It does offer personal assistance, gift wrapping all year long, magazines that—until I started putting them on the shelf—I had never heard of, and a two day turnaround on most special orders. We offer a 20% discount on *New York Times* bestsellers and on books read by local book clubs. But more importantly, and the reason for my being hired, it is local and downtown and willing to put forth the extra effort to locate that wanted book for its customer, even if that means going online to Amazon, Abebooks, or some other used book connection.

That's why it is MY bookstore as well as where I now work.

Now that I am working at the store, I listen a bit closer to the programs on NPR. I often have listened to an interview on "Diane Rehm" or "Fresh Air" and then run to the store to ask Anne to order a copy of the book just discussed. For some strange reason, I think I am the only one who does that! How presumptuous. There are many others out there just like me who also discover a treasure on the radio.

These days, following a book discussion I put the title and author on a list and bring it down to the store to double check that we have it on the shelf or to mention we need to order at least one copy because someone will be in wanting to buy it. As the end of the year draws close, many radio programs and newspaper and magazine articles are noting the "Best of" in fiction and non-fiction. I try to make a mental note, as there will likely be customers coming in asking for these books.

This is a different world for me. Rather than read a text and prepare myself for discussion or analysis, I now need to be up on many types of books; not just the ones that pique my interest. I look at this as a bit of a challenge and count myself a novice in this area.

On the other hand, my knowledge of books related to my teaching career gives me a helpful edge. When a customer comes in and asks for a book for a young boy I often bring them to the shelf of Gary Paulson books, especially *Hatchet*. One thing I learned in the classroom is that girls can handle reading a book with a male protagonist but boys have a difficult time reading about a female protagonist. The Richard Riordan "Percy Jackson" books are also worth a gentle nudge. They bring in Greek mythology in a contemporary setting. Matching a book to the customer is a fun challenge.

* * * *

As one ages, New Year's Eve no longer retains the glitter of the holiday in one's youth. Previous eves found me surrounded by friends standing in the glow of a bonfire built on the shores of Lake Michigan with a potluck warm in a little hut lovingly labeled the Ottawa Beach Yacht Club. The club was the place where my Aunt Effie's previous attempts at teaching me how to play poker at the age of nine began to show signs of sticking in the old noggin. The guys were very patient with my learning the various hands one could hold and which hands could win the pot. There would be a table spread with food and drink.

In recent years I prefer a quieter New Year's celebration at home. Having a dog that has a difficult time with the sound of fireworks also makes the debate about going out or staying in a bit easier. Not having to worry about the other guy or gal behind the wheel as I make my way home following the festivities also plays into it. I have never felt the need to watch *Dick Clark's*

Rockin' Eve or see the Times Square ball drop. I tend to play some quiet music or watch a film. Boring? Perhaps. But I don't have to please anyone but me and in that instance, I am the one who counts.

Resolutions aren't something I make. The way I see it, either I am going to make a change in my life or I'm not. I don't need a holiday to help me decide. I know what I need to do to improve my health, my finances, or make my dreams happen. The experts say it takes thirty days to form a habit, allowing for that change to become part of one's routine. Resolutions are usually broken in the first ten days.

However this past week it seems making resolutions are all anyone wants to discuss. Even Dr. Oz was interviewed on NPR. He suggested making resolutions on the buddy system, especially in the area of weight loss. Losing weight is definitely not one area where I want a buddy. I don't need the extra guilt when I reach for that slice of cheese and cracker.

In recent years I have tried to eat local more often and also discovered the books of Michael Pollan. I follow his common sense mantra, "Eat What You Like but Less of It. Eat Greens Mostly." It also makes sense to shop only the outside aisles of the grocery store which contains many of the items (produce, meat and dairy) that are not processed or full of corn syrup. Pollan noted that our grandmothers would not recognize many of the things we eat. Choosing to eat things grandma might know is a healthier alternative to what many large food corporations offer to us consumers.

January

The Day After New Year's

The winds moaned their winter welcome
as the dog and I donned our morning gear.
All night they had announced their late arrival:
"We're here. We're here!"
As we head east, trees once bedecked with lights
and ornaments, decide to join us.
They spin down the street,
dancing to their own song,
little dervishes in some religious frenzy.
I wait to see if Miss Gulch or a cow might pass,
caught in a winter tornado on the way to Oz.
                January 2, 2012

    New Year's Day. Tess got me up at 5:44 AM. Even though the fireworks disturbed her beauty rest, she was ready to greet the day. What would I do without her? Eleven years ago my collie, Chloe, passed away the week after Thanksgiving. I spent days and months after that staying late at school and finding reasons not to be home. By the spring break holiday I was a mess.
    I called my mom on the telephone, crying "My house feels like the Taj Mahal!" I live in a two-bedroom

bungalow, and that is a bit of an exaggeration. Still the house was lonely without the presence of Chloe. I had no one to step over as she laid in the doorway, no one to say, "You already had a biscuit" as she begged for "just one more."

I'd been in contact with a breeder earlier in the year who had an expectant collie and I telephoned her to see where things stood, since her dog's due date had passed. In a rarity, her collie threw a singleton that the owner decided to keep. She was sorry, but before hanging up did give me the name of a woman in the Detroit area who not only raised collies but judged at prominent dog shows. Carole in Detroit then gave me the name of Jan Blythe, in Mason, who she knew had a recent litter.

Within I week I had Tess. And within another week I remember telling my mom, "I got my life back."

Unlike most women my age, I didn't follow the prescribed societal pattern of college, marriage, employment, and children. It just didn't happen. Still the urge to have something to care for and love cannot be denied. Growing up on a small farm meant that we had dogs. Many of them were dropped off at the side of the road, unwanted by whoever opened the car door and let them out. A dog is much like a child. So when the urge for children was felt, I got a dog.

One does not need to have children of one's own in order to love and care for them. When students would ask why I wasn't married or why I didn't have children, I would often respond, "I do have children! I have you. I give birth to 144 of you each trimester as I love and care for you all day, and then send you home to your real parents."

* * * *

The year of 2011 could be labeled a "downer" if one paid attention only to the last months when so much violence held us staring at the television. Before 2012 began, I had made my decision to retire from the classroom. The final months of my teaching career were marked by the beginning of a new year. Beginnings and endings all at the same time.

The decision made it easier for me to spend those last few months of teaching parting with files, books, movies, posters, and other props used to grab the attention of my students. Slowly the cupboards began to empty out and post-it notes with names of students or teachers who wanted to claim a memento were placed on the back of posters still taped to the wall. I didn't take anything down from my walls until the last exam was given and those students left the room. I didn't want to give them the wrong impression that I was eager to leave them. It was a subterfuge, since behind the cupboard doors were only textbooks. Personal items were already packed away for the trip home.

Teaching became easier after I decided to leave in June. What might the administration do should I stir the scholastic waters? Fire me? Not that I stood before my students as a rebel, but I could pay less attention to what the State was going to require of teachers in the future allowing me to teach those final months with ease.

I didn't have to worry about the data I would need to collect to prove I was capable of teaching children. My view is that such reports should never be asked of a teacher. Data only tells the observer that a group has proven they can jump through required hoops. It does not tell the observer what the group will take from the experience in a classroom or out into their lives.

The final school year was a GREAT school year that deserved these capital letters. It was that good. My seniors were eager to grow and learn how to make that leap into the next phase of their life, and my sophomores were genuinely sincere and honest. Each of my classes—all eleven of them—was a small family. No one was a true behavior problem.

Yes, there were incidences and students who did not perform at the level at which they were capable, but the outside forces causing these incidences were recognized and efforts were made to try to rise above them. Senioritis and family issues can be a stronger force in a one's educational career than I or anyone can fight against. But we didn't go down without a fight.

* * * *

When I look back at those six months of 2012, I see my taking the summer break as usual and then searching for something to take up time in a 24-hour day that can appear too empty, making it seem longer. The position at Windmill Island was an experience but I wasn't a good fit despite having admired the docents who gave tours at many of the historical sites of my childhood—Williamsburg VA, Monticello, Mount Vernon, the areas around Boston and Philadelphia. I thought these guides so wonderful and they are, but it's not the right job for me.

The bookstore seems to be a good fit. I once courted the idea of owning one, positioning it in a nearby town that was without one. I had the site picked out and everything. I think I knew it would never come to fruition as I am not a business person and I'm severely lacking in math skills. The holiday season gave me a full taste of a bookstore at its busiest and I survived.

The Downtown Business Association holds events throughout the year that add some spice to the daily running of the store so it doesn't get boring. There are "regulars" that come in who I am getting to know. Some come every day to buy their paper, or once a week or month to get a particular magazine. Mr. Mendez was in the store while I was sharing a story about my taking students to Paris one summer and now refers to me each day when he arrives as "Paris," just as he calls Lisa "Hollywood" for having left California to come home and take over the store.

I don't know if this is where I am supposed to be but for now it feels good as I make my way through this first year away from my teacher's desk and textbooks.

* * * *

A little dusting of snow this morning. When Tess and I got out for our first walk there was some on the steps. As we make our way from the steps down the patio walk to the driveway, I cut a path with my shovel. Then we continue the path down the sidewalk, resting the shovel against the fence at the end of our property. On our return from the park, I unleash Tess and finish up the clearing of the sidewalk, the driveway and the patio walk. I didn't have any place to go so early in the morning but I was all bundled up so why not extend the exercise a bit and clear up nature's nighttime remnants?

My neighbors tease me about my "neatness." That's what happens when one is a bit anal-retentive. I don't like ice buildup, nor do I particularly like ignoring a situation until it becomes more serious. It is easier to keep up with a situation than try to get oneself out from under it. Exercise is exercise whether one is shoveling two inches of snow or six, and shoveling smaller amounts is easier on the back. I would typically get up at 4:30 AM to get ready for school, but knowing we might get a dumping I would get up a tad bit earlier to shovel before walking Tess. There were times while outside in the silent dark that I would have preferred a snow blower to make the task easier. But when I think of the noise and the smell of the gasoline exhaust, the quiet shush of my shovel remained the easiest choice.

    I once wrote a poem about such a winter day. Over six inches of snow fell on a Saturday morning and the time to clear the path took over an hour. I jokingly thought of this task being a man's job, with me taking on the role of the demure woman inside the house looking out with a cup of coffee in my hand. There are only a few moments such as that one when I think it would be easier to have a man around the house. Not that a man wouldn't be welcomed; there just hasn't been one to dare tackle the job.

* * * *

Thoughts While Shoveling Snow

Snow has grown in my yard overnight.
A squirrel, awake as early as myself,
balances on the telephone wires
chucking and chattering his discontent
with the cold as I dance with my shovel
across the width of my driveway.
I stop, rest my gloved hand on the shaft tip
and look up, seeing him against the gray of this early hour,
all the windows in nearby houses still vacant of light.
For a moment I feel his disgruntle.
I look down the drive toward the street,
glance back at the garage and note how little I have done.

I think of the poet, Jane Kenyon, and her life on Eagle Pond,
How she and her husband, Donald Hall, used the snow to provide insulation,
shoveling it up against the base of the farmhouse.
She wrote that winterizing the house took more than a month
and was more than putting in windows. They needed that first snowstorm.
Then they would retreat once the drive was clear
to their offices and huddle at their desks
near the kerosene heaters to write. Cats would lie on their laps
warming their thighs and purring with contentment.
They would listen for the sound of the plow
to drive by and look out from frost-framed windows to see their mailbox saved for one more day.

I think, "I need a man." I have been shoveling for an hour to only clear half of the drive,
and I want a man to be doing this.
I want to play the role of diminutive female, standing by the window
with a cup pf coffee in my hand, staring at a guy lifting this snow.
I, of course, will have that look on my face that says,
"I feel your pain. You are sooo sweet and strong,"
promising him a warm mug of coffee when he comes in.
And I do feel the pain, ache, rather, running along the base of my back
and my arms near my breasts.
Yet, I keep moving and conceded: "I have a better chance of buying a snow blower

than getting a man to shovel my drive."
I have now cleared three-quarters.

I think, "If this were a weekday, it would be a snow day."
But the way my school district works, I wouldn't know it was a snow day until the drive was cleared;
which it is, and I walk back up along the house.
Looking back, I note other yards are still unmarked—
no paw prints, shovel scars—pure.
A faint drone echoes up the street and is getting louder.
I see two plows, one behind the other, throwing snow from the street up into the yards, and they breeze past mine.
A mountain of compacted snow lies at the bottom of my drive.

I think, isn't this beautiful!"

1-22-05

* * * *

On the fifth day of the new year, the sun is shining brilliantly. I take Tess out for our second walk earlier than usual and discover the light is deceiving. It may be a clear sky but there is a cold breeze. I hurry her along, making plans for a work day inside.

The sun has put a spring in my step. I decide to use this energy to sort through the clothes in my closets and analyze their potential use in this new phase of my life. While I can still wear many of the clothes I wore in the classroom, there are some items I know I won't wear to the store or to church or anyplace else. The task doesn't take long as some clothes are seasonal and I need to wait until the season arrives to decide if I will be wearing them again. Still, I managed to fill the box I liberated from Dykstra Post and Home with some spring jackets and other items that, looking at them now, makes me wonder, "What was I thinking?" in purchasing them.

    I like to shop at resale shops for a good portion of my wardrobe so I don't feel too bad when I toss into the box a top I bought for $5.00 and never wore or wore only once. I still have some feeling of regret, having been raised to not spend money unwisely. "Frugal" was an F word used often in our house.

    My niece, Crystal, and I try to spend one day a month together checking out resale shops and antique malls. Some of our favorites are in Rockford, Grand Rapids and, when we are up north, in Traverse City. My needs aren't many, but Crystal has managed to find some great name brand buys for wedding dresses and sports clothing. Most recently she needed a dress for a Christmas wedding in which she was the matron of ceremonies. She found a White House/Black Market dress for $35.00. When she got home and online, she found it was worth $178.00. That's my girl!

    When I take a break for a bit of lunch the sun shining through the windows still has me in its grasp and I decide on a salad of spring greens, red pear, feta cheese, roasted walnuts and a raspberry vinaigrette. It just says "spring" to my taste buds. Tess is never happy when I use a vinaigrette dressing. I let her lick the bowl when I am finished eating and the sour taste of the dressing isn't pleasing to her palette. Oh well, I can't please her all of the time.

* * * *

I am not the only one who notices that our winters are not like winters of the past. News reporters have been commenting on the subject for weeks as our snow levels continue to drop from the expected averages. I remember my mom talking about one winter when she and my Uncle Blaine were walking home from school on top of snow drifts as the plows had yet to go down South Shore Drive. They had to stop at the home of someone they knew from church who invited them in to dry out as their snowsuits were drenched from sweat and snow.

I asked my mom if they knew the family well, and she said, "No, we just saw them in church each Sunday." Rarely would something like that happen today. We teach our children to not to trust anyone who isn't family and even family members can be questionable.

January of 1978 was the last real storm I remember. There have been bad storms, but in 1978 school was closed for two entire weeks due to the amount of snow that fell during those couple of weeks. Once I started teaching I heard stories from other teachers telling tales of those who managed to get to Chicago and flew down to Florida, knowing school would not be called back into session until the middle of the month.

The 1978 snow was piled so high at our house that my brothers would walk the roof until mom heard their footsteps. By the time she was booted and had her coat on, they were playing King of the Hill and as noted by my diplomatic brother, she had no proof they were where they didn't belong as she hadn't *actually* seen them. The look on her face still reinforced her point and there was no more walking on the roof...for a while.

There were no hills by our house so sledding wasn't something we could do but we had an alternative. My brothers would take out the riding lawn mower and tie the sled to the back of it and pull us down the road.

The winter of 81-82 was also a year when storms came every weekend, closing school each Monday. The entire month of January had four-day weekends. I was a sophomore in college at that time and we were still required to attend classes. We would bundle up looking like Randy in *A Christmas Story*—"I can't move my arms!"—and cross campus only to find a note on the door stating the professor couldn't make it in to teach.

Snow days are just as treasured by teachers as they are by students. If there was a hint that one might be called, I took work home to correct. I also would suggest to students that assignments would still be due upon their return to class no matter what day that might be, making sure not to jinx the possibility of one by actually saying the words "snow day".

My only complaint about snow days is the time my district waited to call one. By the end of my teaching career, our Superintendent was more generous in making the call but the gentleman before him waited until the last second for his call. One time I had driven the twenty miles north—it took an hour—only to find when I pulled into the school parking lot school had been canceled called five minutes before. A mixed feeling of anger and happiness accompanied me on the drive back home.

* * * *

I just finished reading *The Windward Shores* by Michigan author Jerry Dennis. The essays explore the winter seasons up north on Lake Superior and along Lake Michigan and the bays of Traverse City. I have spent many a summer in Traverse City and a few visits in the fall but rarely have I traveled there during the winter months. One of Dennis's last essays speaks to his experiencing a "Siberia of the soul" and my thoughts immediately went to Melville's *Moby Dick* where Ishmael claims his reason for going to sea is the "November in [his] soul." I love that phrase used to describe Ishmael's feeling of melancholy. The reader might conclude the character believes this dulling of the senses will be lifted by some excitement at sea. Little did he know.

The gray skies of winter can create soul-affecting feelings, but we are currently in the midst of a January thaw with temperatures heading to the upper 40's and lower 50's. The sun is shining and all of the snow on the ground nearly melted. Tess will like that. The current snow had crystallized into an icy crust that hurt her paws. I have tried in the past to get her wear booties during these cold months but the look on her face when I put them on her is, "Really, mother? Seriously? You expect me to go out looking like this? No!"

The Siberia or November of the soul can really be a deterrent to daily living and it can sneak up on one so quickly. A snow day where one chooses to spend the entire, or at least most of the day in bed, can be a well-deserved treat. Too many days of those treats creates a habit one finds difficult to break. I must admit, when I left teaching, I worried about such a habit forming for myself. It has not materialized. One reason, a lack of snow. The more dominant reason, Tess. It is hard to stay in bed when a dog needs to be walked. Bless you, God, for this 50 pound gift of fur and slobber!

Sometimes I feel sorry for good ole' Melville. Having taught his tome for several years, I found his personality interesting. It is no wonder that he and Nathaniel Hawthorne were friends when Hawthorne lived in the Pittsfield MA area. They were both Eeyores.

Still, Hawthorne's reasoning was a bit more understandable. Imagine having your great-great-grandfather be stupid enough to buy into the theory of witchcraft and send 19 people to the gallows and condemn poor Giles Corey to be pressed to death. I would have gone a bit further than to add a "w" to my last name thinking that might draw attention away.

While Hawthorne suffered the sins of the father, or should I say, great-great-grandfather, Melville's issues were financial. His father lost his job with its substantial income, and Melville never managed to recover from his father's lack of familial support.

The literary critics refer to both Melville and Hawthorne as being anti-transcendentalists, explaining their negativity as opposition to the transcendentalist theories of the time that life is great. Hogwash! These guys were gloomy Gusses and they seemed to enjoy wallowing in their self-pity. I think they enjoyed the "November in [their] souls" and they had each other to share the grief. Biographies note they did little to alter their personal reflection on life. Perhaps there weren't enough self-help books in the area.

* * * *

I have just finished watching *all* seven seasons of *The West Wing.* My neighbor and I began this little marathon in late August as a way to acknowledge the final weeks of the presidential election. There wasn't much on the television I found as enjoyable as those episodes of *WW*.

I found it amazing how often what took place in the fictitious world of the Bartlett administration was ringing true in the current Obama administration. Often I, or my neighbor, would say, "I hope Obama is watching this." The show, meant to be a reflection on the Clinton administration, made me appreciate those who work in DC. Some people have said, "You couldn't pay me enough," when I would tell them I was a teacher. That sentiment rings true for me in regard to those who work in federal government positions.

Despite that, I am addicted to the news from Capitol Hill, trying to be available to listen to Wednesday afternoon programming on NPR's "Talk of the Nation," which they call "The Political Junkie." Still, I would not like to deal with all the back-stabbing and positioning of politicians eager to rise up in the political ranks.

One episode of *West Wing* has the House Speaker constantly changing the percentage points of tax cuts and various other restrictions on the budget, thinking he has the ability to play a high stakes power struggle game. After President Bartlett states the changes are unacceptable, he stands up from the table and says, "Shut it down," meaning the government. The entire government remains shut down for two weeks until the Speaker caves and a budget is reached. I remember when such an event happened in the Clinton years. It was interesting to see how each party created the "spin" to make the opposing party the enemy.

The fruit of the Aaron Sorkin show that invented banter known as the "walk and talks" left my neighbor and me with memorable lines we often use ourselves. One of my favorite lines, attributed to the character Josh Lyman speaking about character Toby Ziegler, is calling Toby a "doorstep darkener"—referencing his gloom and doom opinions. From one Jewish boy to another the name calling hit the mark without sounding anti-Semitic. The term "doorstep darkener" could also be used to describe Melville and Hawthorne.

* * * *

Death doesn't send a notice telling us when it will arrive at our doorstep and there is never a convenient time to entertain its visit. Nor does it make a difference whether that death is in human or animal form, it still hurts. I received a telephone call from two separate friends in a matter of days telling me they needed to put down their dogs. One due to cancer, the other having suffered a stroke. One was ten and the latter, fourteen.

As I expressed my sympathy for their losses and listened intently to them, I began to think Tess was living on borrowed time. I had been told the average life of a collie is eight to ten years and Tess will be turning eleven a few days from now. I recognize she is no longer the the collie I brought home in April 2002; she has her arthritic aches and there are times when she experiences a senior moment, getting up and heading toward the kitchen only to stop and question where she is going. Often she continues and heads to her water bowl but there are other times when she turns, walks back to her spot, circles and goes down into her mound with a sigh as if to say, "Whatever."

* * * *

It's official! The warming temperatures of the past week have created our first January thaw. I take this opportunity to go to the cemetery and retrieve the Christmas wreath I placed on my mom's grave. When I get home, I get out work gloves, wire clippers and my yard waste container and begin to disassemble two of the wreaths I had for the season. I plan on leaving the one on the front door hanging just a bit longer. It looks good there and it makes me smile when I see it.

Snow certainly covers a yard's worth of sins. My back yard looks very sad with its wilted leaves, mashed plants and overall dismalness. Still, I have an urge to go out and dig, weed, and stand at the border garden sidelines and offer encouragement just like a sports coach. It looks like my rosemary plant may make it through the winter. It managed such a feat last year and is so big now I may have to replant it to a larger section of the herb garden. The warmth in the air makes me want to go out and do something—plant pansies, put down mulch, put spade to borders to create a better yard line

—something! With this urge I do the next best thing—purge.

Every spring my niece has a garage sale. This year I think I may be able to provide her with more than enough items to aid in the raising of three children. Our deal is she gets the items, takes the time to price and sell them, and then the money earned from my share of goods goes towards school clothes or camp funds. Earlier in the month it was the closets; today it is a bureau and buffet drawers. I pull out every piece of clothing from the drawer creating a pile threatening to slide off the bed and onto the floor. Tess, wanting to help, skitters out of the room after a second thought. This is no place for her right now.

Each item is held up, and I question, "When was the last time I wore this?" If the answer is less than a year, it goes back into the drawer, saved for another day, but if the answer different, I fold it up as best I can and place it in the box. There are some things that pull on the fashion heartstrings but just as many items make me cringe. "Hold firm, old girl, and dump," I tell myself.

The buffet is a harder task. I begin by wrapping up a set of eight mugs and dessert plates given to me by my paternal grandmother. She gave them to me when I was still in high school and in the 35 years or so since then, I have never used them.

At some point sentimentality needs to give way to space and simplicity. I realize I cannot hang onto every item for purely sentimental reasons...hit the play button on the song, "I love you ....for sentimental reasons." Sorry. Some of this stuff has to find a new home in someone else's life. I wish them much happiness. By the time I am ready to quit I have a box of clothes and a box of various china pieces to make someone this spring think they got such a great deal.

* * * *

The weather people are finally projecting some truly measurable snow this weekend. As much as it has been a joy not to shovel as much and as often, I wonder what this lack of snow will do to the level of Lake Michigan this summer and how it will affect the farmers and orchard growers.

Some folks project that we will have another early spring, creating the early blossoming of orchard trees as happened last year. I don't know what to think about such proclamations but I know that I have been realizing how spoiled we have been in recent years. While areas of Texas, Oklahoma, and Nebraska have had drought conditions over the past three years, we have been very fortunate.

Michigan does not get earthquakes, hurricanes, tsunamis, and rarely a tornado. It has been quite a time since we have even had blizzard conditions requiring the shutting down of highways. Nor have we had awful ice storms as have been happening in states along the East Coast. By the grace of God we have been very fortunate. Perhaps I should stop writing and go find some wood to knock on.

I have not taken for granted the condition in which I live my daily life. I have a roof over my head and it is mine. I own it; no one can take it away from me. In the past ten years I have put a new roof on the house, put in a new furnace and while doing so, added central air-conditioning. The exterior of the house has been sanded down to its original cedar siding, re-calked and repainted with paint guaranteed to last for twenty-five years.

I don't intend to brag here, there have been trade-offs. I don't have children to clothe or save money to put through college. I don't have a husband with the things a husband requires. (If I did have a husband, however, there would be the extra income.) The point I am trying to make is I haven't had to share my income with anyone else. My income met my needs and I didn't have to think about anyone else when I cashed that check.

* * * *

One month into winter, it finally decided to show up. This morning I woke to two inches of snow on the ground with more arriving all day. I shoveled before I walked Tess, shoveled when I arrived home in the afternoon from the bookstore and then shoveled once more in the evening before calling it a night.

While there are some who wait until the snow stops to go out and shovel or snow-blow their drive, I feel the need to stay on top of the situation by shoveling in small doses.

The weather man said Holland received at least five inches today; which in the big scheme of things isn't all that much. It isn't enough to close the schools. What might give school superintendents pause is the wind chills. While the temperature outside is 10 degrees, the wind chill is 8 below zero. Tomorrow there is a projected high of 13 degrees and there will still be a breeze, meaning more below zero wind chill temperature.

Tess seems to be enjoying the snow. When she was younger she would bound and bounce through it but now she walks with a determined gait through it. She walks as if she owns the neighborhood. There hasn't been much need for salt on the roads or walkways so I don't worry about the pads of her feet yet. I am cautious. She won't wear little snow booties that some suggest for dogs. I cannot imagine how they must feel on her feet and no amount of my talking to her would convince her to give it a go.

Tess is stubborn. I once bought her a yellow rain slicker to wear on our rainy day walks. When I put the coat on her, buckled her in around her tummy, she just stood there with that "Really mother?" look on her face. She is quite good at giving me that look. It's much like the look I got from some of my girl students when I would suggest something that to me seemed totally plausible but to them would be the ultimate in humiliation. Tess, however, doesn't have the ability to roll her eyes.

We do need the snow. The lake levels are down to their lowest levels in over twenty years and I am sure the snow and cold temperatures must be good for the farmers and orchard growers. It is the wind I could do without. That howling can be very disconcerting and make getting to sleep as well as staying asleep difficult. The other night the wind just blew. The news stated we had 51 mile an hour winds here in town. When I woke in the night I thought how difficult it will be to walk Tess in the morning and it might keep folks from getting to church. But when I got up Sunday morning and stepped out from the back porch, I t was silent. There wasn't a breeze to be had. I murmured one of my "Thank you, Jesus. Thank you, Jesus. Thank you, Jesus" prayers.

I have a hard time praying those prayers people pray in the morning or at night. You know the ones that sound as if they were scripted. When I try to pray at night, I fall asleep right in the middle of praising or thanking or asking for some care or concern to be met. So I don't do those types of prayers very often. I guess I'm not very good at those.

What I do better is a more conversational type of prayer. I have a conversation when I'm in the yard, walking Tess, or driving somewhere. I thank God for the beautiful trees in the park near my house and acknowledge their age as a mighty wind leaves many a small branch strewn about its base. I praise God for the rains in the spring, even when they do make Tess a little smelly when we come in from our walks. That rain is what greens my lawn and feeds my garden. I question whether I am doing the right thing at a given moment and eventually I make a determination once I have had the conversation in my head. And more often than not, I thank God when his answer to me is "No."

There was a school year when one of our English teachers was planning to retire. He was not only the department head, he also taught AP English, a course I badly wanted to teach. I made my desires known to my associate principal—that I was interested in both positions—but was assigned neither of them. I was deeply disappointed. I felt I had the leadership skills to be the department chair, and I also thought I had the knowledge to teach the advanced placement class.

Instead I continued to teach the classes I had been teaching for the past ten years. It took me a long time to work through the fact that I had been passed over for these positions. I wondered what I was lacking rather than seeing the gifts I was bringing to students who were taking the general education classes. AP students are an interesting breed. They do their homework most often without question. They have always done well and would continue to do so. The students I had required more of my passion towards American literature and writing to see how they could be successful at it and why it was important for them to do well. My style of teaching was more beneficial for the students I was currently teaching and it was there that I needed to be. My prayer's answer was a "No" in that case, and I realized that was the right answer.

During the winter months when the drive up to Grand Haven would be more treacherous than in the fall or spring, I would often break into a "Thank you, Jesus. Thank you, Jesus. Thank you, Jesus" when I managed to get by a semi that was driving a bit too slow or when a semi passed me and sprayed my windshield with slush making it difficult to see for a brief moment.

I became a granny on the road in these early hours, staying in my lane and only moving out into the passing lane when I had the time and patience to pass. While other trucks and cars were passing me by, I kept my steady pace and often saw a few of those vehicles spun out in the median or along the ditches farther up the highway. Driving early in the morning during the winter months is one thing I do not miss about teaching.

* * * *

It's a snow day for the local schools. As I was out walking Tess I heard one of the girls across the street try to convince her mother school had been canceled. She was telling her mother she received seven messages on her phone telling her that school was closed, but mom still seemed skeptical. I am amazed at how quickly we have gone from watching the television with bated breath, hoping to see our school scroll by. Now there are robo-calls to parents, and even the news stations are sending text messages to our phones letting people know they can go back to bed. I saw my school scroll by when we returned in from our morning walk about the neighborhood. We didn't go to the park this morning but stayed on the sidewalk and checked out a block.

It is cold. Even wearing my gloves made of thinsulate, I felt my fingers begin to tingle with the bitter temperatures. I put Tess back into the house and cleared the driveway, the sidewalk and the sidewalks of my closest neighbors. It didn't take long. Then I came in for a cup of the coffee percolating in the pot on the kitchen counter.

Last night one of my nieces called asking if I thought schools might be closed today and I really thought not. We have received a steady snowfall of about eight inches but nothing that could not be cleared off quickly. It was the temperature and wind chill that made me hedge my claim. I really couldn't be sure. By noon today the local news station said at least one hundred schools are closed, not necessarily due to the snow but to the cold air. Tonight friends from Chicago are driving up on business. I would hate to have to make the trek but am sure they will take their time and arrive safely.

* * * *

It's been snowing for four days now. This is a light snow; even though it has been quite steady I would say we've only received a good foot I have managed to stay on top of the shoveling. Every time I go out I give the driveway a pass with the shovel taking off an inch or two.

The temperature is what keeps many inside. Today the weather people project we will reach a high of twenty-two degrees; downright balmy compared to the single digit temperatures of the past three days. Add the wind and the fact that wind chill has been below zero at times. I have only been going out to walk Tess and to work my hours at the bookstore.

Inspired by a note from Coach Stop Farms I decide to cook a pasta dinner of Trader Joe's chicken sausage with apple, some of my butternut squash from the freezer, onion, garlic and parmesan cheese. I missed this concoction with penne pasta as I didn't have the pasta that I would have preferred. I cut the sausage on the diagonal and the squash was already cubed.

I paired this with a cabernet sauvignon from Charles Shaw, otherwise known as "two buck Chuck" for at one time it could be purchased at Trader Joe's for only $1.99 out in California. Now don't get excited people, there is no Trader Joe's on the west side of Michigan. I need to make what I refer to as "my Trader Joe's run" about six times a year to make my various grocery purchases. The most recent rumor as to why there are only TJ's on the east side of the state is due to the many grocery stores that already exist on the west side. We have our Meijer, and the family of Spartan stores: Family Fare, D&W, Glen's, Plumb's. We do have Aldi's which is also a grocery chain that is run by the brother of the owner of Trader Joe's. Still, they aren't Trader Joe's.

Coach Stop Farms is a local farm in neighboring Zeeland that organically raises chickens and their eggs, cows, pigs, and lambs for processing. They farm with Friesian draft horses. I brought home my first collie, Chloe, from Darryl and Connie's farm and each year I purchase half a leg of lamb from them.

One article that gave the farm kudos was actually about a restaurant in another nearby town, Fennville. *Salt of the Earth* uses only locally grown products for their fare and they work hard to procure these products within a one hundred mile radius. When cabin fever begins to set in, the owners and Matt, the head chef, hold monthly dinner events that not only highlight various meats but local wines and beers as well.

* * * *

These past days I have spent the time reading the poetry of Maxine Kumin and Wendell Berry. For some reason I am unable to focus on a novel right now. A poem provides special insight in a brief amount of words, and one can spend hours long after reading one deciphering its meaning and phrasing. When I do get my mind ready to wrap around a novel I plan on reading *The Roots of the Olive Tree*. This story focuses on five generations of women living in California on an olive farm. The women range in age from 112 to in their 30's. Imagine the conversations which span those years.

The full moon appeared last night but it has been waxing for a couple of days and its brightness has caused havoc through the night with Tess's inner alarm. For the past couple of mornings she has been ready to begin her morning ventures anywhere from 4:15 to 4:29 in the morning. When I is awakened at these early hours, I remembers the times exactly. I took her out for her last potty call rather late last night while I shovel "one last time" and that managed to reset her clock. She slept until 5:59. Thank you, God.

This morning another four inches graced the driveway. While I shoveled, Tess positioned herself at the base of the driveway in a grand posture similar to *Olympia* by Eduard Manet. She just laid there basking in the early morning, looking out onto the street as little flakes drifted down onto her fur. What a diva. She waited, I shoveled and then we set out toward the park

The sidewalk plow had been through so our trek was clear up to the point where she needed to divert into the park to do a little discreet business, which I promptly retrieved into a little baggie. The place was beautiful. Puffs of clouds sat on each branch waiting for the tiniest whiff to push them off a branch and onto the ground. Our only accompaniment was the sound of snow plows scraping nearby driveways. That juxtaposition to the otherwise quiet morning was not like a John Cage piece; it was perfect in its acceleration into morning.

* * * *

The first days of snow have gone away with another January thaw but only for two days and now we are back into the white world of winter. Just when I thought there may be very few school closings in the area we have had three. The second school closing was Monday due to freezing rain, and for some strange reason it brought me to the emergency room. I didn't fall or anything of the sort, I apparently had an anxiety attack. I don't know if this incident was the bottom falling out as my neighbors projected, but the good doctor— and he was a good doctor—asked some very insightful questions as to what might be causing my anxiousness. He did not make any diagnosis but he did suggest perhaps my identity as a teacher and the fact I am not teaching is akin to a mother having her last child leave the house.

My identity *is* in question and I need to reconcile my new life with my previous one. I often bring up the fact that I taught school in conversations, mentioning it as a way of vocalizing the absence of it. Now I need to identify myself in another form. The doctor's critique of my "crisis" may be spot on.

As I shared his opinion with friends they all could see his point and were quite impressed with his bedside manner. I will watch myself very carefully and work towards this reinvention of my identity with open eyes and an open mind.

* * * *

Finally I received word that Jon Meacham's book, *Thomas Jefferson: The Art of Power*, is available for me to sign out from the library. Often I had hesitated in making a purchase of it from the store as even with my employee discount I asked the question, "Would this be a book I might read again?" The answer was always "Probably not," and I just looked at it with anticipation and waited for the call from the library.

I immediately dived into it and am enjoying the book immensely. Having been to Philadelphia and Monticello at least twice in my memory and to Williamsburg twice as well, I could envision Jefferson in these spaces.

One chapter spoke of Patrick Henry's famous "Give Me Liberty or Give Me Death" speech given at St. John's church outside the limits of Williamsburg, after the British governor had eliminated the House of Burgesses because he feared anarchy. I have taught that speech in American literature and could see in my mind's eye the painting that accompanied the text in the literature book. There was Henry lifting up his gaze and his hand toward the heavens while listeners looked on in various states of "Oh heavens, what have we done?" "This man is talking rebellion!", "Treason! This is treason!" and "Yes, the time is now to act!"

Another area of interest in the book is the relationship between Jefferson and his wife, Martha, known as "Patsy". There is the impression they were truly in love, six pregnancies in ten years, the final one leading to her death, attests to that. Their reunions following his trips to Williamsburg and Philadelphia were obviously amorous ones. And then the kicker–on her deathbed she makes Jefferson promise to never remarry as she wants no stepmother raising the children.

Jefferson's grief was also interesting. He spent months sleeping in the library on a platform on the floor, fainting at the sight of his children, and requiring round the clock observation by his sisters and sister-in-law for the first two months following Patsy's death.

I am now reading about Jefferson's first trip to Paris. There has been much said about this time period and I am anxious to match what films and other books have projected based on Meacham's apparently impeccable research.

February

We begin the longest shortest month on the calendar (February always feels long to me) with a foot of snow. It is beautiful morning but chilly. I shovel the drive and sidewalk wearing the long black coat I wear to church to protect my legs from the chill. I am not yet tired of shoveling; it is still a game about how many times each day I shovel and how clean I can keep the drive.

The gentlemen in their top hats out in Pennsylvania have said Punxsutawney Phil, their groundhog, has predicted an early spring—in six weeks! Just be patient. In six weeks it will be March 21st, the vernal equinox and spring. How amazing is that ground hog!

We haven't had a February thaw but did get another foot of snow. It wasn't the lighter flakes of the past; this batch is wet and heavy since the temperature was around the freezing mark as the flakes fell. It took a bit of heft to lift the shovel and, following the plows pass-thru, a good 45 minutes just to clear the base of the driveway.

For the entire time I was huffing and puffing, I was also thinking about how this was the first time I really had to struggle with the white stuff. I was also wondering if some of the schools would have to make up for the fourth snow day. Most schools only allow three school closing days in their calendar.

Last night's storm is now on its way to the East Coast. On arrival, it is supposed to meet up with another system coming from the south and, as they merge. create a nor'easter. News programs are projecting blizzards and power outages. I am thankful for our smaller storm; I cannot imagine how this will affect those still recovering from hurricane Sandy. Will they ever get a break?

I also heard this week that New York State's governor is asking those who live along the coast to think about relocating. He would like to see the coastline returned to its marshes and wetlands. Hearing this I thought of that scene out of Fitzgerald's *The Great Gatsby* where Nick looks out at the bay and, with a sigh, wonders if the Dutch settlers knew what a gem they had discovered when they landed on Long Island. "They must have held their breath."

I know it will be hard for some to pull up stakes and leave their history. Still, one must pose the question, "Is it worth the constant turmoil and rebuilding to stay here?" The intense weather that has breached the Atlantic coast in recent years is surely a sign that such storms will come again in their lifetimes, maybe even again next year.

* * * *

In spite of the snow, I am experiencing a bit of spring fever. I stopped at the library on my way home from the bookstore last night and signed out five cookbooks. I am getting in the mood for basil, asparagus, spring peas and new ways to prepare them. I took out three cookbooks by Jacques Pepin, *The Tucci Cookbook* by actor Stanley Tucci, and Lidia Bastianich's *Italy in America.* Yes, I lean towards Italian foods and not all Italian food is heavy or all about pasta. I find their antipasti dishes light and just enough for me. Some sound so decadent—prosciutto and figs! Who can resist?

My love affair with cookbooks began with James Beard. In the 1970's, he was asked to write a series of articles for American Airlines magazine. Later these articles were reproduced in book form, *The Armchair James Beard*. Each article covers a simple topic in cooking and includes recipes. The book also shares the story of how Beard developed this love of food as he grew up along the Oregon coast.

After reading many of Beard's cookbooks, I followed up with M.F.K. Fisher, who also cooked with seasonal foods accompanied by interesting stories of her life. Her chapter, "How to Cook a Wolf" is a portion of a earlier book she wrote to share ideas on how to prepare meals in a time when typical food stock items were limited, as they were in the 1940's when flour and butter were rationed.

My interest in the story behind cooking recipes began when I discovered Gladys Taber, the original Martha Stewart. Following a university teaching career, Taber began writing a column for a ladies magazines and gained popularity in the 1940's and 50's. She wrote from her home in Connecticut, called Stillmeadow.

Taber would share stories of what she cooked, for whom she was cooking and why the occasion was taking place. It could be just a neighborly visit or it could be a weekend visit of a rather prominent guest. She had many friends who were rather famous authors themselves, such as Hal Borland. In addition, she would share the comings and goings of her life out in the country, raising cocker spaniels to show and being a widow raising a daughter. Her books have been hard to locate in used bookstores or in online sites but I have managed to rack up a nice stack and return to them often.

Just when I think I belong in New England rather than living along the shores of Lake Michigan, another huge storm comes in to that region and reminds me I am best right where I am. Last night the blizzard that merged between the southern front and the western front dropped 34.2 inches of snow in Milford, Connecticut, 29.8 inches in the Boston area and 25.3 inches in Portland Maine.

I cannot imagine shoveling that much snow from my drive. Most amazingly, the East Coast snow all fell in one night! Yes, Michigan is where I belong. We have lake effect snow, but I cannot recall anything like those numbers. Still, think of the stories folks out East will tell of the Blizzard of 2013!

The snow we are currently getting is what I call 'spring snow'. It has a different scent than December or January snow. It isn't as sharp and dry but rather moist with a hint of dirt that promises a thawing—and soon gardens to till and plant. I know this sounds funny, but it is what I smell and it gives me hope. The few remaining weeks of winter will go by quickly and soon there will be forsythia and daffodils.

* * * *

Last night I took Tess for her final walk after spending the day shoveling. Over a foot of lake effect snow fell here. As we turned the corner Tess noticed the shadow coming towards us before I did and she slowed her pace. It was Lauren, our neighbor four houses down, who also felt compelled to go for a walk. So compelled in fact, that she began walking without stopping by the back door to deposit the brown egg she had just retrieved from Penelope, one of her four chickens. That egg looked safe nestled in the palm of her wool mitten.

The city of Holland doesn't have an ordinance about chickens. Cory and Lauren just asked each of us in the neighborhood if we would mind their getting a few chickens for the back yard. There would be no rooster, they assured us. Their home is in an area behind the garage and on occasion one hears their cluck but only when things are absolutely quiet.

As Lauren held out Penelope's egg to show me, I commented on the wonderful taste of organic eggs. My brother, who lives north of town, also has several chickens. He also named each of them and the birds respond to their names when he calls them in at night. The yolk of an organic egg supersedes all other egg yolks. There is nothing more golden. It is richer looking and makes scrambled eggs that are a true delight to see upon a white plate for breakfast—or any time of day.

Just as I have found in the past, this February has felt like the longest shortest month of the winter. Only a couple of days before the month began, our first winter snow hit and it seems it has rarely stopped. Weather people project another storm arriving on the 27th.

March begins at the end of the week and that means spring is just around the corner. In two months I will be sweating and grunting as I throw down mulch in the gardens and Penelope and her girlfriends will be producing more eggs as the days grow longer and the temperatures rise.

March

It's here! March has come in like a lamb. The sun is shining, the roads are dry, and I've just returned from going through a car wash. Weather-folk are projecting four days of no precipitation and sun! There is still plenty of snow in the yard and drifts that make turning a corner a bit testy, but I know that in 30 days there is a strong chance I may see grass.

* * * *

The second day of March and I'm sitting on the enclosed front porch, a south facing porch, with the door open to the rest of the house, enjoying my own little happy hour. I have a nice glass of cabernet sauvignon and some crackers with red pepper hummus as a respite. I was not a fan of hummus until a friend shared this brand with me last week. I was immediately hooked. This dip will definitely be a part of my patio soirees in the future.

The eaves drip as the snow slides down and melts off the roof. I expect it all to be gone by tomorrow, as another sunny day is being projected. It is still cold. The temperature dangles around 30 degrees. This keeps the roads dry. The snow piles in the yard are still chest high and they could still be here come the first day of spring; but by then, they'd only be as high as my ankles.

Easter is the last day of the month—early by my standards. I've pulled out Spring decorations but it is hard to match them to the view outdoors; pastels and floral against a backdrop of drifts. I'll try not to look at both together too often.

Tess is asleep on the rug on the front porch. Sun shining through the window panes creates a pattern on her fur. She is recovering from a bit of an intestinal infection common among dogs who take walks as we do. She eats snow from the drifts on our walks as well as smells and gets close to the leavings of other dogs, so this infection did not surprise the vet when we went to see her yesterday.

It was our first meeting with Dr. Kendra Wolk. She and her husband are in negotiations to purchase the vet clinic from the widow of my previous vet. John Schmidt was a remarkable doctor. He had been my vet for over 34 years and saw me through the lives of my three dogs. I was spoiled by this man and didn't realize it until after his death from a heart attack. He never charged me for an office visit; in fact, I never realized there was such a charge until my first visit following his death. He only billed me for tests and medications if needed, and often gave Tess bags of treats in addition to our meds.

Dr. Schmidt died in his sleep one September night. I learned that he had a weakened heart when he prescribed a heart medication for my previous collie, Chloe. As I inquired about the medication when initially prescribed, his response was, "Audri, it's the same medication I'm on." That told me he truly cared about what he gave his clients and how he prescribed it.

He may have had a physically weakened heart, but when it came to caring for animals, his heart was larger than life. People would find hurt animals and drop them off for John to rehabilitate. Just prior to his death he was trying to save the life of a hummingbird, taking it home in a shoebox and hand-feeding it sugar water throughout the night. The bird didn't survive but not for John's lack of care and trying. May Dr. Kendra prove to be just as caring and may all of our animal family members be under the care of such devoted doctors.

* * * *

We mark daylight savings time today and, in all honesty, I really don't get it. I think that farmers either get up earlier to go out into the fields or stay out later in the fields. A day still has only 24 hours. Was there really any need to tamper with perfection?

Tess, however, is a daylight savings time dog, at least this year. She wasn't her usual alarm clock self this morning. When I woke, it was 6:20 AM, a full twenty minutes past her usual, "Mom, it's time to take that walk." In fact, when I prodded her to join me she gave me a look from her dog bed as if to say, "You go, and let's say we did it together. See you when you get back," and rolled over.

I'm glad she's feeling better after her urinary tract infection.

The warmer weather has reduced the drifts from shoulder high to waist high to knee high and little edges of grass are peeking out beneath them. Tess likes that. She doesn't have to go into Rin Tin Tin mode to find a spot to do her business. The 70 degree days we experienced last year is the topic of much conversation on the news programs as they compare it to our normal temperatures of upper 30's and low 40's.

I can handle it. All things in their time. It can be so easy to rush through life. Reminding myself to slow down and enjoy now can be tricky with so much happening and so many things becoming obsolete as soon after they hit the mark

Cell phones, for instance. No sooner was the iphone invented than out came the iphone 2. We're now up to iphone 5! Is that really necessary? What happens to all that plastic hardware? What landfill does it find itself in? It scares me to think how we will be defined by the things discovered after we are gone.

It is actually interesting to discovers things that were buried. I think the previous owner preferred to live her life as sparingly as possible and a garden of any kind was too much "work" and not enough beauty as the by-product. When I dug up the edges of the yard to create border gardens, however, I found little shards of dishes, not many but some; nails, small bolts and one tiny clear bottle.

All this talk of digging gets my fingers itching for yard work. Take note of it now because later I will deny I said it. With the temperatures just above freezing, the snow melting, and sun shining, I have begun "the list". My list compiles spring and summer jobs that need doing. I try to do them before mid-June when things heat up.

By the end of April I hope to put down fresh mulch in the gardens and prepare the raised beds with additional soil and compost. I never got those things done last year. I was so busy wrapping up the school year and then the heat wave hit. In addition to yard work I need to do some painting as well.

The steps leading up to the front and back porches have taken a beating from being scraped of snow. They will need to be repainted. That too, will get done early. I want the outside jobs finished before I tackle interior ones, since the exterior is the most visible. The kitchen will need to be repainted, a job that requires some scraping and plastering before I actually put paint to brush.

Right now the kitchen is yellow. I didn't do anything to it when I moved in, but I really don't like yellow. People say the kitchen should be a bright color like yellow but they don't live in my house. I am leaning towards a soft gray to off-set the red Formica countertops that were the selling point for me when I looked to buy a house. I want the countertops to be the focal point of the kitchen.

* * * *

Some of this spring fever is natural but it could also be a response to my year of change and redirection. At a recent church meeting I shared the experience of my anxiety attack and Dr. Hoey's assumption of its cause. One of the members, Kathy, later emailed me with a suggestion of a get-together with some friends who are also experiencing a re-direction of their lives.

Kathy's best friend from childhood recently moved into Holland; another left a special education teaching position in South Haven due to fatigue; still another was experiencing a new teaching position and an empty nest as her daughter moved out.

I thought this could be a wonderful way to meet other women who are going through changes in their lives. Many times we keep our angst to ourselves as we think no one will care or it is too trivial a matter. I asked if I could invite another friend of mine who not only retired from teaching at Hope College but also, after close to 30 years of marriage, lost her husband to multiple myeloma.

When we arrive, wine bottles in hand and additional noshes to add to the table, Kathy shares her news from earlier in the day: being diagnosed as a diabetic. No wine for her. The table of treats is filled with a variety of mini cheesecakes and I find myself thankful I brought bowls of dried fruit and almonds for finger food.

Knowing little of each other we begin to talk. One thing women do well is talk and find common ground. The hours full of laughter and genuine questioning and concern go by quickly. When we leave, my friend tells me she has not laughed as much as this evening since the passing of her husband. I am grateful I thought to ask her to join us, and hope we can continue this little group of women looking for direction.

* * * *

The fact that it stays lighter in the evening makes leaving the bookstore feel strange on the nights I close—as if I am cutting out early. When I began working in November, the nights grew dark by 5:00 PM. It feels magical in a way, as if there is still more wonderfulness in the day to behold. I am ready for that wonderfulness.

It is the third day of Spring and we are still getting some snow, so the temperatures are far from spring-like. I've been invited to a cousin's home for dinner and I'd like to dress in bright colors or at least something other than a thick sweater, but the charcoal gray sweater tunic with black leggings draws me in and seems more appropriate to going to a home along the lake. Warmth reigns over fashion as wells as what the calendar says.

I've already trimmed the ends off a pound and a half of green beans to make green bean almandine as my contribution to the chicken dinner. I am craving spring so I grabbed the bottle of Peninsula Cellars 2011 pinot grigio from the refrigerator and open it. In the glass it is the palest of yellow and when I place my nose over the glass I inhale the scent of pineapple and the memory of last summer when my niece Crystal and I went wine tasting on Old Mission Peninsula, just outside of Traverse City.

The crispness of the wine makes me want to gulp but I refrain. I forgot how good it was when we tasted it at the winery. I drink in those days last June before it got so hot. I take the glass out to the front porch and drink in the day's sunshine as well.

I've just finished reading *American Terroir: Savoring the Flavors of Our Woods, Waters, and Fields,* by Rowan Jacobsen. So I wonder how the scent of pineapple, a scent I equate with more tropical climes, found its way to the soil of the upper portion of Western Michigan. Looking at the wine, it is a beautiful soft color. Tasting it, the crispness crosses my tongue and almost makes me sense a sparkle in the bottle, but no.

The area around Traverse City has at least thirty wineries. The geographical location, the 45th parallel, if traced east to Europe, follows a line that travels through some of France's best wine country. Thank God, someone made the connection here in Michigan and took the dare to plant grape vines in addition to cherries, apples, apricots. Next to cherries, wine is the second commodity to come from the Leelanau and Grand Traverse counties—and it wasn't affected by last summer's heat wave. The grapes were saved.

* * * *

We enter holy week with the celebration of Palm Sunday. This still feels a bit strange with the morning temperature being all of 28 degrees. Still we grab our palm fronds and parade through the church to the delight of the little ones in the church community. The cry of "Hosanna" takes on a new meaning for many parishioners when it is revealed it means, "God save us." We are in such need of being saved from ourselves—and our politicians who have forgotten the oath of office they took and revel in partisanship (at whose expense?).

Listening to the news can be discouraging when doing what is right fails to take precedence over doing what will keep congressmen funded by lobbyists. I long for the days of Edward Kennedy, Gerald R. Ford and Robert Byrd. They understood that the word "compromise" didn't necessarily mean "giving in and forgoing conviction" so much as meaning "what will best serve the most Americans."

I was too young, a pre-teen, to understand the sacrifice President Ford made when he pardoned former President Richard M. Nixon shortly after he assumed the presidency. "Our long national nightmare is over," he began and continued to explain how this act would move the country forward at the expense of his own re-election. He fell on that sword so that America could get out from under that dark cloud and get on with the business of being a nation. We need more presidents like Ford.

* * * *

I read in the local newspaper this morning that one of my former students and his entire family were in a serious automobile accident this past weekend in Iowa. The family was bringing my former student back to college following his spring break. Everyone was injured, my student's girlfriend was killed, and the driver of the vehicle who crossed the line into their lane also died.

My heart aches for my former student. Not only will he have to heal from physical injuries, but the emotional injury of his girlfriend's death will leave a deep scar. How can it not? I have heard of such accidents, but never one involving a person I know. Knowing enough about Colin's character, I think this young woman must have been quite unique and special.

So what does one do when feeling helpless? I reach out to my church and ask for prayers. I write my former student a letter letting him know I am here should he want to connect. Then I go into the garden. I cannot do much to immediately ease Colin's pain, but I can see the results of my energy's use in the garden beds as I pull out the dried rosemary that failed to make it through the winter, cut back the fronds on the tarragon and lavender, and give the soil a bit of a scratch to awaken.

Earlier this month, I took down the last holiday wreath and set it on the back fence to wait until a warmer time to take it apart arrives. With the sun now warming the driveway, I take out my pliers and pull back the prongs holding the evergreens in place. As they release I place them in the yard waste container for compost. I cannot justify putting the wreath in the trash when, with a little extra effort on my part, I can dispose of it in a better manner.

Now that the past five days have been sunnier, although with below-average temperatures, I feel putting my spring banner out is a bit more appropriate. It *is* spring, but now it seems to actually begin to *feel* like it.

With Easter, flowers appear. I have a beautiful lily on the dining room table. There are pansies in ceramic galoshes on the front porch, an array of other spring blooms in a pair of metal galoshes on the back porch. I love rubber boots or "willies," as they say in the UK. With my pair, I can walk through any puddle with Tess and never fear wet feet. I harken back to my childhood rubber boots and raincoat as I played outside the barn at home. Tess, on the other hand, comes in with muddy paws that require washing On many mornings, I hold in mind an image of Martha washing Jesus's feet just days prior to his going to Jerusalem. It isn't really the same but it makes the task less a task than a privilege, mine to care for a pet that has brought me such pleasure over the years.

Last year I played the Easter bunny in the neighborhood, placing a basket of candy-filled plastic eggs in the backyards of some of my little friends. We had had an unbelievable warm spell with temperatures in the 80's. All the snow had melted and the holiday came a week or two later than this year.

Now, without being too obvious, I try to get a glimpse into these backyards to see if they are conducive to my fun this year. I think by the end of the week the temperatures are supposed to be up in the 40 degree range, worthy of children collecting a candy-filled egg or two wearing a spring jacket.

April

      I put the shovel away this afternoon – no foolin'. Even though there were still some snowflakes coming down, they were not living very long on the ground. It was beautiful. The back porch and garage are all tidied up as is the small hosta garden along the patio walkway. I do need more mulch and, so the project doesn't look only half-finished, I scattered the remaining bags along the raised bed walks. I will still need two more in that area as well. So I'm off to the hardware store again!

      Thirteen more bags of mulch, two cubic feet per bag, should be enough to cover the last border, leaving three bags for the garden walkway. As I place them along the border I get a bit worried. Did I miscalculate? We'll see. It amazes me how quickly a bit of grass sprouts its little head, even if it doesn't live long. I pluck it from the softened ground and toss it in the bucket. It has been raining all week but I am determined to finish laying the mulch.

      I could easily fall prey to the gray skies and cool temperatures that might lead me to sit in the house and moan about not getting in the yard. I refuse; laying down mulch is a much easier task than one might think when temperatures are cooler. No sweat is dripping down the back of my neck and no patches of moisture are showing under my armpits.

* * * *

It has taken me a day to really absorb the Boston marathon bombing. I am saddened that some people in the world want to hurt others for no reason other than to prove they can do it. For us, in the United States, this type of unthinkable violence is new, but there are many countries whose citizens face this sort of violence every day. It has become a part of their world. It's not a club in which I want our country to become a member.

The resiliency of people present at the marathon is inspiring. When the bombs went off, instead of running away, many turned and ran toward the blasts to aid and assist. I was reminded once again of a scene from the TV series *West Wing* where, as the president is heading to an event to make a speech, he heard of a bombing which took place at a college swimming event. It would have been impossible for President Bartlett not to have mentioned the event in his speech. What he noted were the fellow swimmers who left the safety of where they were to run into the fire to save whoever they could. As he stated, "They ran into the fire." I hope I would have been such a person, able to show such courage.

Having been to Boston more than once, I have always admired its history of patriots who fought against tyranny. The marathon bombing occurred on Patriot's Day, a day Massachusetts sets aside to honor those women and men. That the women and men of Boston did not forgo their historical breeding, but ran to assist, makes me both esteem and admire them. I find myself even wishing *I* was from Boston.

I was a history minor in college and had parents who took us to historical sites on family vacations, I was thankful when each of my nieces and nephews took me up on the offer of a trip to visit such famous sites when they turned 13. My three oldest nieces all selected the Boston area for their trip. We, along with my mother, walked the Freedom Trail, visited the Old South Church, and climbed aboard the USS Constitution. We also visited other areas—Concord with its various authors and Plymouth Plantation. We went whale watching along Cape Ann and, as we left Massachusetts, spent a night in Stockbridge at the Red Lion Inn with a visit to the Norman Rockwell Museum. I feel an affinity for the state and New England in general.

The daughter of a friend of mine, a science teacher at the high school, lives and works in Boston now. I immediately called Scott when the school day was over and the final bell had tolled. He was still reeling himself at the danger his daughter Courtney had been in, as she was at the finish line. She only felt the blast and was not physically hurt. But the memory of the event will likely linger forever. One of the high school English teachers often ran in the marathon and I managed to get an email to him. He was not in Boston this year. A blessing.

I was touched to see on the news that at the Yankees game in New York City, the flag of the City of Boston was raised; and that during one of the innings, "Sweet Caroline," the theme song of the Boston Red Sox, was sung. There are running groups around the nation, who ran in the name of Boston to show that they are undaunted. One local running group wore shirts reading "Run for Boston."

Boston needs our prayers. Its citizens know the world is watching and they are showing the world they will not be left cowering; they are undaunted. As I write, the bombers have not been caught and the horror is still alive.

So what to do with a mind considering the answers to life's deepest questions? Work it off. The projection for rain today won't come to fruition until the afternoon so I decide to put another notch on my gardening belt.

With Tess at my heels we head outside. Walking the yard, we rake up any dry patches and areas where crabgrass has decided to take hold. After scraping away the dead grass and placing it in my bucket, we scatter grass seed. There are more spots than I anticipated and I need to make another trip to the hardware store as I have no seed left for the area between the street and the sidewalk. That patch is incidental but it important to the first impression of the exterior of a home. It could lead one to question, "If this is left to look so awful, what might the rest of the yard and house look like?" An hour later, the weeds and dry grass are in the waste container and patches dark with moisture and seed are just waiting for that projected rain.

This has been one of the wettest and coolest Aprils on record, diametrically opposed to last year. Severe storms are on the docket for the next two days, complete with thunder and lightning. Many of the rivers are above flood stage, and news programs have shown area residents parking their cars away from home and using small boats to get to the cars and go to work. There is a strong resolve among these people who choose to live along the river for the beauty of doing so, knowing the trade-off is yearly flooding. I often wonder what washes up on the shore once the river has receded.

We are all tired of the cool damp days, longing for the spring we expected, but soon they will be days of the past and we will have forgotten them as we relish in the warmth and sunshine.

* * * *

I attended the local high school's Café Pops concert last night. The program promised an evening of light classics and jazz. It was a nice respite from all of the harrowing news of the week; to sit down at a table with a friend, sip a cup of coffee, nibble some cheesecake and listen to young people dedicated to the art of making music. My neighbor, Jared, is a cello player in the chamber orchestra. His orchestra played three numbers: Ralph Vaughn Williams' "Rhosymedre", Gustav Holst's "St. Paul's Suite Finale–Dargasson" and Richard Meyer's "Vanishing Point." The first two pieces were so mellow and soft, very relaxing; and the final piece was a bit contemporary but still delightful.

The jazz band played some classics, "Come Fly with Me" which always makes me think of Sinatra, and an arrangement of the Lennon/McCartney tune "Blackbird." The members of the various orchestras waited on tables while another orchestra was playing. They held a little raffle during a brief intermission. It was nice to see parents and grandparents come out to support their children and the arts.

The arts are often one of the first areas of education to be cut in a school system. I had recently heard the Ionia School District will be cutting it from their elementary program in the fall. How can we create and stimulate new artists if we do not introduce students to music and art while they are young? They are even eliminating their physical education program, and yet the United States has a severe problem with obesity.

What the school has decided to attempt is to use the various talents of its classroom teachers to keep these programs going. All of the "specials" teachers will be laid off. I don't know how many times I have heard educators say that the arts help students in areas of math, etc., and here we are, taking away one more tool for student success.

When I arrived home, I quickly walked Tess one last time for the evening. It was snowing. In mid-April! I turned the TV on to discover they found the second suspect in the marathon bombing in Boston. The first suspect was killed earlier in a shoot-out with police. All day the city of Boston and its neighboring suburbs were shut down as the police searched for this young man.

When the area police gave notice that area residence could come out while using extreme caution, one resident noticed blood on the side of the boat he had stored in the driveway and immediately called 911. Officials found the suspect, alive, but barely, as he had been shot in the shoot-out as well. I had so hoped they would find him and arrest him rather than have him die as his brother did.

Hopefully he will recover and give the police the answers they need in order to understand why these two brothers decided to set off bombs at the Boston Marathon. Such an act needs to be explained.

* * * *

I love waking up to the sound of chirping birds. It's an important signal of spring, and also tells me the first walk of the day will be a dry one. Fortunately there have been dry moments among all of the rainy days of the past two weeks to allow for me to walk Tess and come home dry. Nothing is worse than a wet collie. Although she handles it well, it takes her hours to dry no matter how many towels I use to get the initial rain wiped from her coat.

If the morning chirp is the sound of spring, the first cut of grass is the scent of spring. It may take a few more days or a couple of weeks before that happens, but it too is a good harbinger.

This morning before heading up to Grand Haven to meet other retired educators for coffee and a chat, I planted pansies in the flower pots. They will sit on the porch steps adding a bit of color until the peonies and irises bloom. In recent years I have found an orange colored variety and it adds a fun contrast to the deep bluish purple variety I usually pot. I have placed them in ceramic orange pots that dot the steps and draw the viewer in.

Only this morning, with hands in the dirt, did I realize it could be considered a take on the colors of the national flag of the Netherlands. Orange and blue are also the school colors of our local college, Hope College, founded by Albertus C. Van Raalte and other Dutch settlers. I also noticed a bit of giddiness as I worked with the pots and plants in my attempt to make my home and yard looking fresh for spring and outdoor entertaining. It felt the same as when I don the yards with pumpkins in the fall.

My new neighbor began to move into the house next door last night. Mark is young, only 21, but I admire his tenacity in purchasing a home at such a young age. Most young adults are still trying to figure out who they are and what they intend to do with their lives. Owning a home requires taking on a great amount of responsibility.

This young man already appears to have made those decisions. He immediately came over and introduced himself, again a good sign, as young people tend to keep to themselves and require being approached as opposed to approaching. Our houses are located on the boulevard portion of the street which does not allow cars to be parked in front of them, so I offered my driveway for him to park his car while the moving truck took up his drive.

Once the truck left, he immediately was over to retrieve his car. Again, a sign of responsibility. I must admit that I too at times fall prey to negative assumptions about young adults simply due to their age. The media enjoys the titillation of showing people behaving badly. Perhaps it is the Lindsey Lohan effect. That poor girl can't seem to get out of her own way to save herself, and whoever is advising her needs to do a better job of it. To become the laughing stock of late night comedians and cause eye-rolling among news reporters is a hurdle she will find difficult to leap over.

I moved into my neighborhood in 1994 unfamiliar with living within city limits, having lived in the country since I was five. I didn't have to retrain myself in the ways of respecting my neighbors and maintaining a modicum of quiet. It was quiet at the farm. Our only neighbors were childless and lived an eighth of a mile down the road. When my family first moved in,, the road ended at our driveway.

As a child, I got to understand the words of e.e. Cummings' poem *Just Spring*—"when the world is mud-luscious." The road to our house oozed with mud so thick, shiny and enveloping that my parents had to park our car and truck at the neighbors while we walked to our house until things dried out. My mom made several trips from the car to bring home groceries and clean laundry as the water table was too high for us to use the washing machine.

The neighborhood was different in '94. There were very few couples with young children. Now we have sixteen kids whose age ranges from 16-and-driving to seven months.

The neighbors of the past kept to themselves most of the time, an occasional hello or wave safely from behind a car window and driving away was all I got. The exception was one couple who, like me, had no children but had a dog. Hydrant, a Dalmatian became the best friend of both my collies; first, Chloe and now, Tess.

Chloe was older than Hydrant when we moved in and the first to part company with her. Hydrant lived until she was 17. And although she had a strong heart, the rest of her body was giving out. Hydrant had issues with many dogs, especially black dogs. She was very territorial. For some strange reason, Hyd didn't see

Chloe was a threat and the two bonded, hanging out often when we were all outside. We even had sleepovers when Hyd's mom and dad went out of town.

When Chloe died of a heart attack at 13 and a half, Hydrant didn't flinch when five months later I brought home a little fluffy baby named Tess. In fact, Hyd took over some of Tess's instruction. She taught Tess how to fetch a toy and how to cover another dog's territorial pee with her own. It was quite an education to see this in process. It has been over a year and a half since Hyd was put down and Tess will still look for her upon occasion when entering my neighbor's house.

Young couples and children change the dynamics of the street. The teenagers ride their bikes and play catch in the boulevard while the tots follow their parents throughout their yards with tot sized rakes, shovels, etc. depending on the season. Their presence in the neighborhood made Halloween so much fun as they arrived dressed in a variety of costumes.

Young moms gather to pass off clothes and advice on separation anxiety and daycare. In July we gather to have a neighborhood potluck making the area feel like a community within a larger community.

I hope new neighbor, Mark, will feel a sense of belonging after he is fully moved in.

* * * *

The perpetual spring has ended and we are now leaning towards summer, or at least the temperatures and sunshine make it feel that way. These last days of April are finally cheering the neighborhood. The children are out in the yards and riding their bikes up and down the boulevard. Parents are pulling the younger ones in wagons towards the park.

I have already met my April goals for yard work and am now waiting for the time when I can plant tomatoes, eggplant, peppers, squash and the annual herbs of basil and rosemary in the raised beds. My excitement about yard work and garden preparation had me forgetting about screens and storm windows.

As we arrived at our first seventy degree day, that need came to the forefront. Down into the basement I went to haul out the screens. In no time I was climbing up ladders, taking down storm windows and putting in the screens. I can still do this task and wonder when the windows will get to heavy or worse, my ability to balance will require me to ask for help. With the windows back into the basement, I began to haul up and put out the patio furniture, raising the umbrella to air.

Later in the evening while taking the garbage to the street I was asked by neighbors if I will host an early patio party this weekend as it will be the first Friday in May. If the weather stays as beautiful as it is now, I don't see what could prevent me from assenting a month earlier than usual. The heat of last summer forced many of them to be canceled as folks found comfort in front of their air conditioners.

It happened earlier than I imagined—I gave the lawn its first haircut. All the rain and now the warmer temperatures have made things pop, including my lawn. The leaves on the trees are beginning to unfurl their baby growth and it reminds me of a Monet painting as the landscape is a bit blurred by this gentle stretching of leaves. My hostas have yet to emerge from the beneath the mulch. By now their leaves would usually have poked through, but many of the ground flowers and plants are late due to the cloudiness and rain of April.

May

What can be more endearing than to find a little bouquet of heliotrope left on your back porch steps? As I left the yard to take Tess for an afternoon walk, Casper, the little toddler from next door, called my name. As he hung held onto his mother's hand, Susanna said, "He's been asking if you were going to walk Tess." My little friend and I shared a greeting; he pulled a heliotrope from the yard and gave it to me.

I stuck it behind my ear, and Tess and I made our way down the sidewalk while Casper, mom and baby brother, Shepherd, knelt in the yard to examine the flowers. On our return home, as I turn the corner behind my house and onto the brick walk, I discover Casper's gift. The heliotrope now drink from two little vases on the buffet.

This is what living in a neighborhood is all about. Getting to know those who live around you, lending a helping hand when one can and having children see there are other adults in the world besides family who genuinely care. It is about creating a community. Over time, that community changes as families move out of the neighborhood and children grow up, go off to college or get married. Still, it is a community within the city where we look out for each other, or as one neighbor joked when another neighbor stated he didn't have to worry about their house being looked after while they were gone, "No, there are enough Peeping Tom's in the neighborhood to keep an eye on things."

Just the other day, while I was talking with Dori from across the street, the railing on my front porch came loose. After Dori left, I called to another neighbor, Bob, who had built my steps and railing to tell him, humorously, that "I had a screw loose and could he come and look at the railing, fix it, and let me know what I would owe him."

I told him I had to leave for the bookstore, but that I'd put a ribbon around the rail post that was loose so he would know which one had broken. When I returned from work later in the evening, the ribbon was off the porch rail and tied to the front door handle, letting me know he had been there and it was fixed. The next day when he came home from work, Bob stopped by to check and tell me that a little wood putty over the screw would hide the spot where he needed to drill into the post.

Later that night I had one of my first Friday patio parties and felt better knowing no one would come to the front of the house and meet some calamity because of the broken post.

My first Friday patio parties were an idea I borrowed from one of my aunts. As a widowed mom living in Grand Haven and raising two boys, one developmentally disabled, creating a sense of community was very important to her. When she moved into her home on Grant Ave., she went about the neighborhood one late Friday afternoon and invited the neighbors to her home for cocktails. She wouldn't take "no" for an answer.

That was the beginning of many events she had in the community. At her funeral, one neighbor told the story of my aunt having collected the abandoned Christmas ornaments from the city when they were updating the downtown streets for the holidays. She doled some out to all of the neighbors to create their own cityscape. That Christmas they decked their houses with these bells and ornaments one last time in her honor.

My patio parties are more voluntary and usually attract a crowd of regulars. No one is rebuffed for not attending and everyone is welcomed when they can make it. On the first Friday of the summer months at 5:30 PM I replace Old Glory for the evening with a banner that reads, "Wine a bit. It'll do you good."

If the banner is hanging, it means the furniture pillows are on the chairs, there is ice in the large abandoned flower pot for stashing cool drinks, and the beginnings of a feast is on the table.

Dog dishes are set out for those who bring the "entire" family. I originally intended the gatherings to be a happy hour after a long week; my impression of a happy hour being an hour or two, but a fun idea can be hijacked and before you know it, it is 10 o'clock and a good time was had by all.

* * * *

Holland's Tulip Time began in the 1930's when a school teacher named Lida Rogers entertained the idea of Holland honoring its heritage by hosting a festival with the tulip being the queen of the show. I don't know how quickly the idea was embraced but I do know that my family's involvement started when my mother was about five, which would set the year as 1939. I have a postcard showing her on a float in front of the Warm Friend Hotel and Tavern dressed in white top and tights, wings on her back, with a watering can tilted to imply she is dousing tulips; a diminutive spring fairy.

Our family took part in the week of parades. During the Volksparade, we scrubbed streets that the Mayor formally announced were too dirty. In the Kinderparade, we held various items of Dutch heritage as we tried to stay walking in a straight line. Then we'd watch from the sideline as my older brother played either the cornet, the French horn or tuba during the Parade of Bands on Saturday.

Over the years, we have also klomped our fair share along Centennial Park and on River Avenue. My mother and nieces donned authentic costumes, cleared by an evening inspection earlier in the school year, to entertain visitors from all over the world. It was during my mom's years in high school that, as a Dutch dancer, she began to date my father when he offered her a ride home at the end of the evening.

Still, it is the tulips that bring crowds to our town. I have a very close relationship to this blooming bulb. From the age of 13 until I went off to college, I cleaned many of them each summer as my brothers brought them in from the fields. Vern and Ester Veldheer were our closest neighbors at the farm. They ran Veldheer's Tulip Gardens with Vern's brother, Elmer and his wife, Marlene.

When we first moved to the farm, their business was small and in competition with Nelis' Tulip Farm. When the Nelis farm closed, our neighbors began the Dutch Village enterprise. Veldheer's gardens is now in its 65th year of operation, planting thousands of tulips each October for tourists to admire the next spring.

After the festival ends, the tulips remained in the field until June. Once we were out of school, my brothers climbed up on Vern's tractors to dig up row upon row on tulip bulbs. As they bring each species of bulb into the barn, the bulbs are emptied into screen-based frames where the dirt can fall through and the bulbs can dry.

After the bulbs are determined to be dry enough, they are emptied onto a machine with a conveyer belt that moves bulbs through a gentle brushing to remove the thin onion-like skin of each bulb. My job was to follow the bulbs and as they passed down the line, separate them. The smaller bulbs would be replanted in the fall and the larger ones would be packaged, a dozen bulbs per bag, and sent out across the country to the tourists who had purchased them during the festival. While other kids our age picked blueberries to make money, my family cleaned tulip bulbs.

Most schools in the Holland area hold half-day sessions during Tulip Time. In the afternoons, students participate with the bands and floats in the parades. During my years as a teacher, I often thought back to my high school days of praying for rain on Thursday, which would require the Kinderparade to be rescheduled to Friday, resulting in a free Friday afternoon. In my later, teaching years, I'd arrive home from teaching as the parades ended and traffic jams began—parents racing to pick up their children at school and tourists back on the road to the next attraction.

My current participation in Tulip Time has mostly been as a supporter/onlooker when my nieces and their children danced in the park. Grand Haven, the town where I taught, is far enough away to be untouched by Tulip Time. Their festival takes place in the summer when they celebrate the local Coast Guard.

* * * *

Reader's World, the bookstore at which I work, is located on the corner of River Ave. and 8th St. (the main drag of Holland). Anyone driving west to Lake Michigan or north to the other side of town will pass the bookstore. All of the parades pass the bookstore, travelling west down 8th St. and curling around past Kollen Park, ending at Holland High School on the corner of Van Raalte Ave. and 24th St.

The past five days of Tulip Time, with two more to go, brings traffic to the store as folks come looking for a public restroom, asking for directions or about the timing of events in the area. We are ambassadors of sorts. My experience at Windmill Island in the fall has proven useful as I share incidental information such as: the Dutch wore wooden shoes during the work week, saving leather shoes for Sunday because there was a leather shortage; the point on the wooden shoe would denote a fisherman rather than a farmer as the point would be used to hook the net and pull it in; some male costumes are from the same province but one style is the workweek costume while the dressier costume is what one would wear to church; and the Dutch who settled in Holland were like the English Puritans who settled in Massachusetts. They wanted to build a community around their own beliefs.

Last night I had a reunion of sorts. As the street was getting ready to host the over 700 high school students in their Dutch costumes to perform the 15 minute dance program, I noticed two of my former students from Grand Haven looking in the bookstore window. Our eyes met, and I heard through the glass, "It's Ms. Hill!" and in walked David and Iliana with hugs and the question, "What are you doing here?"

David graduated three years ago and had taken over the running of his family's blueberry farm north of Holland while taking business classes at Davenport University in Grand Rapids. Iliana is taking classes at Muskegon Community College. In a sea of strangers, how warm to meet old friends.

Catching up on all of the news that three years apart can create, they missed watching the dance program entirely but didn't appear disappointed. Soon they were off in search of frozen yogurt at one of the two stores which recently opened in time for the festival.

A gentle rain began just as I was closing the store but I had brought an umbrella, having heard hearing on the news that rain was expected. The walk to my car was a bit longer and the Kinderparade was just ending as I was due to arrive at the store, so I asked a friend from church who lived three blocks away if I could park my car in her driveway. My previous plan to walk to and from work was abandoned after hearing the weatherman's report.

Seeing my former students led me to contemplate once again whether my choice to leave teaching was the right thing to do. The students were all smiles and our conversation animated as we relived days in the classroom.

I know I was a good teacher and I love the connections I made with my students. Seeing the light behind the eyes when a student understands what is being taught is one of the grandest moments in the life of a teacher—and I've had to give that up. I do make a connection with people here are the bookstore but for the most part it is a fleeting connection. The daily relationship is created with only a few.

* * * *

Today marks the first farmer's market of the summer season. It always begins the week following Tulip Time, so when I arrived city workers were still removing the parade bleachers from the west portion of 8th Street. Last Saturday's parade of bands withstood rain and chilly temperatures to put the week of festivities to bed for one more year. It is a beautiful morning today, 61 degrees with a slight breeze; the sun is shining down on the market, which is full of hanging plants, flats of annuals and vegetables.

The earliest vegetable on the tables in some of the stalls is Michigan asparagus. I buy a pound to use in pasta, risotto—and I am also fond of having it on slices of toast, covered with a poached egg. There are some stalls selling rhubarb but I decide to wait a bit. My purpose for coming to the market today is twofold. One, I have never had the opportunity to come on the first day due to teaching and two, to buy the plants I need for my raised garden beds.

In the center of the market, anchoring a main corner, is Boeve Farms. I cannot remember a summer when they have not been at the market or at that particular spot. Being handed a tray, I proceed to select my tomato plants, deciding to only buy six plants this summer, each a different variety. First I choose two heirloom varieties–Cherokee purple, a deep burnished tomato that looks more auburn than purple, and Mr.

Stripey, a tomato that will have a yellowish stripe throughout its skin. I select an Early Girl and a variety named Cherry Bomb and round out my six with two smaller varieties–Yellow Pear and Candy. Both will go well on my salads.

Following the tomato selection, I choose a globe eggplant and an Italian variety that will grow in a more elongated shape. I then round out my choices with the purchase of a yellow pepper and orange pepper plant; they are sweeter than the green variety and add color to many dishes.

I had hoped to buy my basil and rosemary but as basil is so sensitive to cool temperatures, I decided to wait. On Saturday when I return I will most likely purchase a basil bouquet and wait until after Memorial Day for the herbs.

I also saw a vendor selling bunches of Tuscan kale. I should have stopped to inquire but I was in a rush to get to Boeve's booth. So anxious was I to buy my plants, my fingers have been itching for days to make these purchases. In the next couple of days I will do some research on the kale plant and revisit it later in the week.

I can't remember when the Holland Farmer's Market began but, following my move into town in 1994, I have been an avid supporter. I believe my purchases have made me physically healthier as I try to eat locally grown, fresh and in season foods.

This is a big change from how I was brought up to eat. We canned tomatoes, beets, and peaches. We blanched asparagus, sweet corn and beans, and made our own strawberry jam. We even had cows and pigs that we sent to butcher; when the parts were returned, we packaged them and put them in the freezer.

Our diet was complimented by canned soups and quick fixes like Hamburger Helper on occasion. These items contained lots of preservatives and sodium to sustain shelf life and they also helped me sustain an unacceptable weight. I sometimes joke that all I need to do is look at a salt shaker and I can put on five pounds. It also didn't help that my mother was mainly cooking for my father and my sports-playing brothers. The family dinner table filled with meat and potato meals, rounded out with rolls and lots of butter and gravy.

On arriving home from the Farmer's Market, I change into gardening clothes. The plants rest on my patio table while I quickly mow the lawn. The night was warm and there was little moisture on the grass this morning. By the time I arrived home, the grass was dry, allowing me time to quickly finish this task that I don't enjoy as much as I do others.

Then it is down to the basement to bring up the tomato cages and the two cages I built to keep local night creatures from getting to my eggplants. The past two years I have had a struggle with furry burglars, be they raccoons or opossums. Finally I went to the hardware store for chicken wire that I turned into two cages three feet high. Once I planted my eggplants, I place these cages over them and dug them into the ground to secure them from being pushed over.

One task in the yard leads to another. After planting my 'crops,' I bring out the hose and twist on the spray nozzle giving them a good welcoming soak. Standing there watering, I notice a weed cropping up, first in one place and then in another. Soon the yard basket is out and I am on my haunches going from garden bed to garden bed, pulling a rare weed and also thinning out my invasive crop of Bouncing Bet.

If I had known this plant would spread so fast and far, I would have given a second thought to planting it nineteen years ago. When I was a teenager, I hated to be asked to weed, but now that it is my yard, I approach the task differently. While doing this task, I can think of other things and still get the job done.

I keep an eye on my watch as I need to retrieve the neighbor's dog from their home at 11:00 AM while a realtor takes customers through their house at 11:15. I am not keen on Steve and Dori moving, but I understand their need to make room for Dori's mother. Their home here doesn't have a bedroom on the main level and Dori's mom needs that.

As we age the tables are turned and we are becoming our parents' caregivers. Their dog Gabe comes over with no trouble, but soon he realizes there are people in his house! Steve and Dori have just returned from spending a week at Disney World. During that time, Gabe stayed with friends who also have a golden retriever.

Gabe doesn't bark but he is clearly concerned and doesn't take his eyes from his house as he watches through the fence. He paces between where he can see the house and my gate, wanting to head home. I offer words of assurance and I think they are working but then I notice Gabe using his nose to flip up the gate latch—and off he trots towards home.

I grab a larger leash and cross the street. I know Gabe is at the back door. He comes quickly to me but would prefer not to cross the street back to my house. He isn't resisting me as much as saying, "Hey, I gotta stay here and protect my home. Don't you get it?"

The realtor isn't there more than another ten minutes. When his car backs out. I tell Gabe we can go back home. He is at the gate, and once out, it is all I can do to keep him from charging across the street without looking for cars.

I stay firm as I tell him to walk and then halt when he gets to the base of my drive. Looking both ways and seeing no cars I say, "Okay Gabe," and he's off.

* * * *

This morning is projected to be another gold letter day–sun, light breeze and temperatures in the low 70's. I decide to take a "Sunday drive" although it's not a Sunday, and head south to the town of Fennville to check on the surrounding orchards. The drive down Blue Star Highway and 58th Street is colored in variations of purple, as lilacs are in bloom. Some appear as an oasis in a field, giving note that once there stood a home that is long gone. The lilac's place tells where a doorway may have been.

There is a slight hill on 58th St. just before one reaches the intersection with M-89. Each side of that street is filled with redbud trees, magnolias, forsythia and lilacs. Turning right toward the west I begin to imagine what the orchards will provide.

As the road turns toward Crane orchards, I see hill upon hill of white blossoms. I am filled with such hope for the fall when those blossoms will become the apples I longed to pick last year but couldn't due to the warm spring in March, followed by the hard freeze in April of 2012. The view of blooms travels up small hills and extends two miles down M-89 toward Lake Michigan. It holds such promise.

* * **

Do you know how you feel when you have been thinking of something for a long time, so it hovers in the back of your mind, constantly resurfacing as you continue to push it back in the file of your brain for another day—and then that thing falls into your lap? That's what happened this morning on my way back home from Saturday's visit to the farmer's market.

I had read in the local newspaper that Third Reformed Church was going to hold a used book sale on Saturday to raise money for summer student mission trips. I left the market and was driving home when I remembered the sale. With ten minutes to spare before the sale opening, I pulled into the church parking lot. Hardly anyone was there. As I waited a few more people approached but the beginning crowd didn't bode well for the sale.

No sooner had I walked into the community room when I spied two books by Joan Anderson—*A Year by the Sea* and *A Walk on the Beach: Tales of Wisdom from an Unconventional Woman.* I had been thinking of rereading these books, along with Anne Morrow Lindberg's *A Gift from the Sea,* over the summer. I had been looking online at the titles from our distributor at the bookstore and been hesitant in placing the order despite my employee discount—and here they were on the table for only a dollar each!

I had just finished reading Melanie Benjamin's book, *The Aviator's Wife*, a historical fiction based on the life of Anne Morrow Lindberg. I'd had no previous opinion of the famous aviator, Charles Lindberg, but this book made me decide he was a dreadful specimen of human being. Lindberg wanted a "pure" family and, after discovering that the Morrow family was, in his opinion, flawed, he fathered seven children with German women following his involvement with the German government prior to WWII. His wife knew nothing of this until she found deathbed letters written to these women in 1974 (the year of her husband's death).

Having read *The Paris Wife* by Paula McLain about Hadley Richardson, Ernest Hemingway's first wife, and *Loving Frank* by Nancy Horan about all the women involved with the architect Frank Lloyd Wright, I put *The Aviator's Wife* in the category of books about deplorable men who behaved badly because they felt entitled. Society let them, along with the rest of their gender, treat women as less than equal. Often these wives were better human beings than the men they married, but had low self-esteem.

At the book sale, I looked around the tables, making my way toward the children's books and there it was: *Cranberry Thanksgiving*! I had been ruminating about this book since the winter months, wondering if I should order a copy in paperback and here this one was on the table in hardcover! And near it, a hardcover copy of Norman Rockwell's *Willie Was Different*.

I have twice been to the Norman Rockwell Museum in Stockbridge Massachusetts. The first time Rockwell's museum was in a house on the main street of the village of Stockbridge. By my second visit, a larger museum was built outside of town. The new museum allowed more of Rockwell's paintings to be on display at once.

I have been fond of this *Willie* book since seeing it on the Captain Kangaroo show. It takes me back to my childhood and I can smell summer breezes and clean laundry on the line.

That's the most wonderful thing about books; they take you places where you have never been or back to places you loved. Unlike TV or films, imagination is a most important part of the journey, as what we envision is our own making, not what a set designer or screenwriter wanted the viewer to see.

To discover treasures that have been haunting my mind for months in one place and for only one dollar per treasure is a delightful way to begin a morning. How can the rest of day top it?

* * * *

It is hard to see parents age. When my mom died in 2005 at the age of 71, she wasn't old, or at least she wasn't acting old. Her death was quick once her breast cancer had returned, only 8 weeks. She went to it with such grace and dignity. As she was dying, she was still teaching me how to be a better human being. My father took her death hard. My brothers and I thought surely he would follow with a broken heart, but instead he holds his heart in his hands daily and grieves a hard grief.

He will be 81 this summer, and he's aging in a way that puts his children and grandchildren constantly on guard. Six months after my mom's death, he had his first fall in the garage. He didn't call anyone, and I found him the next morning with his knee swollen to the size of a basketball.

I quickly made substitute teaching arrangements and called 911. He spent two weeks in the hospital and two months in a nursing home. Naïvely, I thought this would be the end of injuries rather than the beginning.

Since his first mishap, he has spent additional time in the hospital after having forgotten to take his medications. The result was major confusion and more falls. The weekend before Christmas he fell and broke his ankle so badly it required pins, plates and wires to put "Humpty back together again." It also required another stay at a nursing home.

This stay was harder. For my father, nursing homes are places where old people go to die and are forgotten by their families. In some cases, he is straight on and I think that is his fear. He constantly needed to be reminded that his stay was temporary. I brought a calendar so he could cross off the days, but he didn't use it. It had disappeared by my third visit. His daily evaluation of the home where Medicare paid for his stay was always negative.

My Dad's return home was met with relief and excitement. He was anxious to get back to his familiar things and get clearance to drive so he could resume his daily visits to my mother's gravesite. He did allow me to chauffer him to doctor's appointments, etc. while he gained confidence in his ability to get behind the wheel.

But taking car keys away from elderly family members is a tough measure and he wasn't ready to go there yet.

Then, last week my niece found him on the floor of his bedroom and noted he hadn't taken any medications for four days. She had visited just before the weekend to give him a haircut and my oldest brother saw him the following day. When he found himself back in the hospital, my dad himself asked "Why didn't I take my pills?"

As we had watched the EMT paramedical team carry him out of the house, his feet were visible from beneath the sheet. It was the first time they looked so frail, unable to hold up this man who stood as tall as John Wayne.

The toxins and his weakness kept him in the hospital through the weekend and sadly, once again, he is in a nursing home to regain his strength.

This nursing home, however, has wings housing a variety of patient care levels. One wing is assisted living, a second is for my father and others requiring rehabilitation, and the third is for those in their final stages of life. Here, as I walked through the lobby with my brother, I could see patients reading to each other, playing cards. One group was even patting a beach ball in the air to each other. No matter where I looked, the lobby was full of elderly people active in one form or another.

I left that first evening with some hope that my dad would not only get the care he needed but also be encouraged to interact with people his age. He isn't the only one who has lost a spouse and perhaps he can see that there are people who grieve that loss but also can manage it and keep living.

This most recent event has forced me to see my father in all his vulnerability and I don't like it. My father has never been the easiest man with whom to live. I don't know how my brothers feel, but there have been times when I was thrilled to be his daughter and other times when his opinions and behavior made me cringe. Still, he *is* my father and fathers are supposed to be strong, face the tough challenges of life, teaching their children that those challenges can be overcome. Now I see him wanting to succumb to life, withdraw and go "gently into that good night." Not on my watch buddy!

Today I am bringing Tess in to visit with him. He has been asking for her and I was told all I needed to do was show proof of her rabies shot. Last night when I called I was told my dad's attitude was good but he was still weak. I asked for him to be reminded that his stay was again temporary so he needed to work at regaining his strength.

In the meantime we are employing Lifeline, the agency that provides emergency care should he fall, and Visiting Angels, who can come in once a day in-between our visits to see that he has taken his medications and eaten. The driver's license may need to be confronted this time, but I will let my brothers chime in on that call and follow their lead. Time will tell.

* * * *

Memorial Day is the unofficial beginning of summer and in the past twenty-six years it has been a breather before graduation and final exams. It has been a time for making plans to head up north every other year–what to pack? What are we to feed the masses on our night to cook for the family? It is that prolonged weekend which for me is a quiet reflection.

This year, the holiday begins with a run to the Ann Arbor Trader Joes. I haven't been there since early December and I am in need of many items for Tess and myself. I was completely out of any Charles Shaw wine that, even though it is no longer $1.99 a bottle, still goes by the nickname "Two Buck Chuck". As inexpensive as this wine is, it has managed to garner attention in the wine world. It is composed from a variety of grapes purchased from small vineyards throughout California. These vineyards don't have the names of a Kendall Jackson or a Stag's Leap but the determination to produce quality grapes that create a good bottle of wine is important.

With a Whole Foods just a mile down the road from Trader Joe's, it is hard not to stop there as well. I don't purchase much, as I find the that products I would need from Whole Foods can be purchased at home in Holland at a much cheaper price. Still, the store has created a blue cheese dip that I crave.

On the drive home to West Michigan, my neighbor and I stop in Chelsea at the Common Grill for lunch.

Craig Common, owner of the restaurant, was lured into setting up shop there by actor Jeff Daniels, who grew up in Chelsea and runs the Purple Rose Theater, named after his first movie, Woody Allen's *Purple Rose of Cairo*. Daniels wanted a quality restaurant in his hometown for people to patronize when they would come to one of the plays at his theater.

We didn't need a menu, our taste buds were already set for the Common Grill's own gazpacho with lobster spring rolls on the side. One spoonful and it was summer! I could have ended the meal right there with the rolls and soup but couldn't resist the offer from Cheri to split a slice of key lime pie. The little dollop of whipped cream on the top had shavings of lime zest and zing! Summer.

Decoration Day is what this holiday was once called—a day to commemorate those who died in the Civil War. Families, mostly women and children, who were left fatherless would go out to the cemetery to decorate the graves of their loved ones. My grandmother and her siblings always called it Decoration Day, not 'Memorial Day'. Following a visit to the cemetery, grandmother would host the entire family at her home for fried chicken, potato salad, and other typical summer fare. With eleven siblings, their spouses and children, people spread all over her home, inside and out.

Here in Holland today, American flags are out up and down 8th Street. But before driving down to the bookstore, I drove past Pilgrim Home Cemetery where my mom and paternal grandparents are buried. American flags line the entrance and drives throughout the cemetery as well.

Once I attended the service that follows the parade at the cemetery and was surprised to see Asian and Hispanic families with chairs and picnic baskets next to the the grave of their loved ones. Their culture required more than just placing flowers on the grave. They took time away from the everyday to reflect on their loved ones, to honor them by telling stories and sharing a meal in their presence.

Many of my great uncles served in the armed forces during WWII and my dad served in the Korean Conflict, often called the "Forgotten War." Our family was fortunate that they all came back safely. My Uncle George Heneveld didn't even graduate from high school before serving in the war. When he returned home he hitchhiked to Michigan State University to apply to the school of veterinary medicine. They denied his application as he didn't have a high school diploma.

Not to be thwarted in his desire for a better life, he hitchhiked back home and the next day set off to East Lansing again, this time with his service medals for the war. When he went in to the registrar's office he threw his medals on the registrar's desk and said, "Don't tell me these don't prove I deserve a chance." He was admitted on probation for the first semester, graduated and even taught veterinary medicine at the University of Kansas.

Uncle Yutz (the Dutch word for George) was my favorite among my grandmother's brothers. He was soft spoken and kind. I took great pleasure in introducing him to Tess at one of our family reunions shortly after Tess came to live with me. He gave his approval of her and it meant so much to me that he thought her 'a grand girl'.

Because it's my Monday to work at the bookstore, this is the first Memorial Day parade I've missed in a long time. It starts a block down from the bookstore and classic cars are already turning the corner and finding a spot to park, planning to transport veterans who want to be a part of the parade but cannot walk the route.

Volunteers are passing out little flags to those who plan on watching the floats, bands and veterans pass by. There is a young man across the street, about half way down the block, in his finest Marine uniform. I smile to myself as I watch him adjust his cap, looking at his reflection in a store window.

I wonder if this is his first time walking in the Memorial Day parade. He is nervously pacing the sidewalk like a groom at his wedding. I stand inside the store and admire him for his service and his pride in his accomplishment. There are many service people who don't mention they served in the armed forces; not out of shame but humility. They were doing what their country called them up to do.

I also have a friend with whom I cannot share this day. She despises all war. I agree with her in not liking war itself, but I cannot dismiss the men and women who were doing their duty or who joined the service as a means to advance their life dreams. I don't believe Memorial Day is honoring war but honoring the courage and valor it took to participate in it.

The parade whistle has blown and I am hearing the drums of a marching band. The parade must be starting. I hear applause from the sidelines as people honor those who march. My hands always hurt a bit as the clapping never seemed to end. But when I think of how others took bullets, are minus an arm or a leg, or suffer from post-traumatic stress disorder, I figure that I can suffer sore hands.

June

This week marks the last week of school in the West Michigan districts. Many local schools have graduated their seniors and the underclassmen are edging toward freedom as day by day as they cross another exam off their list, returning home by noon to either study or take a nap.

Last year at this time, the faculty and staff retirement parties had begun. I was bouncing between correcting papers and tests and packing the car for the trip north. The consequences of my retiring had yet to sink in.

A year later, I am once again packing to head north but without the family reunion. I will be at Chimney Corners for the week with no one arriving to join me at any point. It will be interesting to see how the week plays out. I am bringing books, including some cookbooks, and without relatives around, the evening meal will be determined by my own schedule and taste buds.

Renting the cottage this year puts me in good stead to rent it again next year when the family reunion resumes. Hopefully, this decision to be up north alone, away from the daily activities of the bookstore and away from dealing with the health issues of my father, will give me the opportunity to reflect back on this entire year.

The idea for this year of monthly reflections was urged on by those who have enjoyed the seasonal letters I write as a way to connect with friends and relatives all at once without having to repeat myself. When someone suggested it, I wasn't sure I'd have anything important to say or if anyone might be interested in my daily comings and goings. Then I decided that I needed to remember what this first year 'after school' meant for me.

What I have discovered is that, when one leaves a profession, the word 'retired' doesn't mean one dries up and has nothing to offer the world. Although my offerings may not be as evident as in a classroom, my position at the bookstore has purpose, and I know that my knowledge of literature is not being wasted.

As is often the case, one of the local high school's AP English classes is requiring its students to read over the summer. Grand Haven High School required this of its AP students as well. It was one way to determine who might be up for the AP challenge, weeding out those students who like the idea of an AP class on their schedules but are not willing to put forth what the course will require of them.

One book is required for all AP students: *St. Lucy's Home for Wayward Girls Raised by Wolves.* Then they can choose from a series of book choices. Many students are not familiar with the novels and some of the staff at the store are not either. Last night while the store was quiet during dinner hour, I wrote up a brief description of each of the additional reading options and placed a + or − after each novel to indicate the novel's interest level for each age group.

For instance, *The Scarlet Letter* is a classic, but the Puritan prose and Hawthorne's writing style can be draining, forcing a student to lose interest in the relationship between Hester Prynne, Roger Chillingworth, and the Reverend Dimsdale, with whom Hester had an affair. The darkness of the novel and the idea that baby Pearl might be possessed by the devil might bring them in, but it is still a difficult read.

When I returned to work I asked other staff if they found the write-ups helpful. Jokingly they wondered if I missed teaching, but found the advice about books helpful—and a surprise they had not expected.

I wouldn't say that I missed teaching, but I can't let what I *do* know go unshared if it can help someone find a good book. I, too, can put down a book that fails to catch my attention, but if I can keep a student from purchasing a book that might not suit them, or introduce them to one they may cherish for the rest of their lives, I feel I am being of the most help.

Even as I finished loading the car, I had a worried sense I might regret heading north. It was an intuitive feeling that something horrific could happen or that

I might be disappointed by the lack of relatives stopping by to knock on the cottage door.

Normally when I head north, the farther north I get the more excited I become as if I am coming home. All my favorite haunts are there for me to visit and see how or if they have changed since the last time I was up. I don't feel that this time. I don't know what I feel—numb doesn't quite sound right nor does relaxed. Still there is a sense I am heading in the right direction.

Sunday morning finds me feeling strange to be up at the cottage alone, with no relative at a cottage nearby or driving up to acknowledge my arrival. Still, after many years of coming north, I have wanted to experience this—up north, alone—and *feel* it. During reunions, the evening meal controls how one spends the day, always knowing dinner will be at 6:00 PM sharp. Today, the first full day at the cottage finds me a bit lost. I will have 24 hours before me with no conditions as to how I spend any of them.

I begin the morning by starting to make a pot of coffee but catch myself in time. On weekends, I always make Chai Tea. I had also planned on making breakfast later in the morning but soon I am sautéing spinach in butter and scrambling eggs for eggs Florentine. By 8:00 AM I am dressed, dishes washed and find myself longing for a Sunday newspaper.

Knowing that few, if any, stores will be open I drive to the grocery store in Frankfort for the paper and then head to the main street to window shop. This gives

Tess a nice walk without too many people on the sidewalks, although she rarely minds the attention they give her. Heading home to the cottage, an impulse makes me drive past it and on to the little village of Empire to buy asparagus from my favorite roadside stand.

Many years ago, I discovered this little stand where asparagus rests in mounds and a little sign asks you to drop $2.00 in the bucket for each pound bought. It was soon added to the list of ritualistic stops I make while "up north."

After getting back in the car I think, "I'm halfway there," and continue on the next village, Glen Arbor. This impulse soon becomes financially dangerous. The Cherry Republic, an empire of buildings which sell all things cherry—jam, salsa, mustard, ketchup, BBQ sauce, chocolate covered, and wine—-won't be my ownfall but the next store on the corner will.

Cottonseed sells my favorite brand of clothing, Flax, and beneath the portico are two racks at 50% off. I buy a dress I had my eye on last year, and a top I had obviously overlooked last summer as I was enamored by the dress. All year long I had been thinking of that dress and now here it is...at 50% off! I'm often called the Queen of Delayed Gratification, and I would say waiting paid off; I buy the dress and the top for less than the original price of the dress alone.

Returning to the cottage, I make a salad of greens, red onion, feta and the fresh strawberries I purchased at the farmer's market on Saturday before I left home, topped with raspberry pecan vinaigrette. I spend the afternoon reading on the porch and take Tess on walks, often noticing the skies darkening to the south. Will rain come? As evening settles in, dinner is another salad of tomatoes, basil, garlic and olive oil. Someone in another cottage makes a fire and the scent delightfully wafts over. Yet, as wonderful as the day was, I still am feeling a bit lost.

I awake early the next morning to the sound of loons on Crystal Lake. Their call is so mystical; only heard up north and in the deepest silence of the morning. While having coffee on the porch I decide once again to visit more haunts. Back to Frankfort I head with the Crescent Bakery in my sights. One fall I came north and stopped in for breakfast. On the menu was a Robin's Egg Panini – eggs, mushrooms, basil pesto, tomato and goat cheese. I became addicted and, like an addict, when in the area I need to get my fix.

Following breakfast I drive out of town to Gwen Frostic Studios. Ms. Frostic died several years ago and despite the little bit of commercialization that has transpired in the selling of her stationary, it is still a stop not to be overlooked. I failed to truly admire Frostic's talent and initiative when she was alive. I was too young to fully comprehend what it must have taken for her to buy this property, choosing to live with nature, and create her art. I only saw her as a woman who made these great note cards and had two golden retrievers named Eliot and Emerson.

When we arrived, we would enter the store and make our way down the stairs to her studio to see if she was in, hoping to say hello and pet the dogs while my grandmother and mom would shop upstairs. Now I see her not unlike myself, one who didn't follow the predominate path in life; after college there was no marriage or children but a full life of creating art.

Another ritual haunt is the Cherry Hut restaurant, in operation since 1922. My cousin, Sharon Spencer, spent her summers waitressing there as a teenager. While she still sees her time spent at the restaurant as a summer job, I see it as one in a long line of reunion memories. I'll never forget the one night Aunt Geneva and Uncle Maurice treated us all to a piece of Cherry Hut cherry pie for dessert. It may not sound like much but there were over 100 of us at that evening meal!

My last stop for the day is the Barn Swallow, an antique store on the grounds of Crystal Gardens. This place is so packed with things to delight the senses that I can go through it twice and still I know I have missed something wonderful.

Today I find tucked in the corner of a sideboard, a white china turkey planter to add to my collection. I love the fact that, because it is white, I can leave it out all year. I am always drawn to the kitchen wares and need to talk myself out of another set of cloth napkins or apron or market basket. I have many of these things and, although these are beautiful, since I fail to use the ones I have at home, it's hard to justify purchasing even more. So, today, it is just the planter...and a pair of earrings for baby Ella who recently had her ears pierced.

When I return to the cottage one of the employees stops on her way back up from the mailbox to the office saying, "You have some mail, Audrianne!" Surprised, I could only think of one person who would track me down and think of sending me a postcard: my friend, Deb. Sure enough. The card was Monet's *On the Bank of the Seine, Bennecourt*, 1868, telling me to have fun. It is just like her to send some "home" up north to me.

With packages brought in, it is back to the porch for more reading—a new book, Joan Anderson's *A Walk on the Beach.* While taking some time away from her marriage, Anderson finds friendship in the company of Joan Erickson, the wife of Erik Erickson. Erickson becomes a mentor as Anderson tries to search for meaning in her life. Almost halfway through I can't help but think of my friendship with Deb. As I observe her marriage I am drawn to the Rilke quote Erickson mentions in the book, "the highest task for two people in a relationship is to stand guard over the solitude of the other." I see Deb and her husband, Louie, doing just that. What a gift they have given each other. They do not fear losing themselves in their marriage nor do they feel threatened by their individual selves. They present these selves as gifts which make their marriage all the grander. Could I ever be that lucky? Is it too late for me?

So soon the week comes to an end and it is time for me to head home. I am looking forward to getting back to my routine at the bookstore and seeing to the care of my father. He will be moving to an assisted living establishment soon; we just have to find an affordable one. I will also make strawberry jam with my niece from berries purchased at the Holland farmer's market.

This has been an interesting week. I appreciated being up north alone but at the same time it was a bit too quiet. I admit, I missed the various relatives making an appearance.

What this teaches me is in all things there is some give and take. It's just like the rest of my life. I don't regret retirement, but I do miss my contact with teachers and my students. In a matter of years I will not be remembered there. Yet the mark I made on those students will help carry them out of the school halls and into the next step in their lives.

Afterward

The first year passed more quickly than I thought it would. I remember telling my seniors to take in everything their final year had to offer—plays, concerts, etc.—because the last year of high school quickly becomes a blur as soon as the homecoming dance lights are turned out. I don't know what I really expected from this year except more time to do the menial tasks I had to deliberately find or make time to do. Often they have been done at a breakneck pace or following a second wind.

Other retired teachers have told me it took them two years to get beyond checking their day by measuring the clock as to what they might be doing in the classroom. I only found myself doing that a few times—"it's 10:00 AM; I'd be finishing second hour soon."

What did sadden me was to hear others in the profession tell me they wished they were in my shoes; the passion for the classroom was slowly draining from their bodies, their spirits damped by all of the negativity and restructuring of curriculum without giving any standards an opportunity to be fully and properly measured. I remember that feeling at times. In the last six years of my teaching career our department had to rewrite the state benchmarks four times.

I have always told my students to follow the little voice they heard when it came to matters in life. Trust instincts, follow passion and do no harm. When it came to careers, I never saw college or a white collar profession for everyone. Much of the country was built by people who worked with their hands and hearts, artists, who were good at what they did. Where would the world be without our skilled mechanics, masons, musicians, and moms?

At eighteen it is difficult to hear that voice when school districts are requiring acceptance into a four-year college as part of graduating, and parents and grandparents expect their child to attend the family alma mater. Where do desire and the little voice urging one to be the best person they can be come into play in life's choices?

I wish I could say I had some secret insight into the choice I made but that would be a lie. I heard my own little voice and following it seemed right. I would also be lying if there weren't times I attempted to look into a cloudy crystal ball for answers.

I still have questions and there are times when I feel insecure about the future, yet I will trust the advice of Maria Ranier Rilke who in *Letters to a Young Poet,* told his young writer to "live the questions". Like my 2012 seniors, I found myself at the edge. I could choose to back away or take the leap. I leapt and the landing wasn't so bad.

Acknowledgments

We're all teachers, it's just that some of us choose to go to school, study the methods and practice of teaching and be awarded a certificate saying that we did. We then present ourselves to an interview committee, and if we prove that we have, as Tom Wolfe wrote, "the right stuff," we are deemed worthy of the school's personal dynamic and given a classroom.

I have been taught by some of the best teachers—Bill Blomendaal and B. J. Berghorst, to name two. Their lessons and personalities are deeply entrenched in my being.

In addition to my teachers, I thank my fellow workers at Grand Haven Area Public Schools and the students I was honored to have in my classes. Thank you too, parents who entrusted me with their sons and daughters.

Thank you friends and family for gentle nudges and words of encouragement. Life-long learning takes some hand-holding. Deborah Noe Schakel, Cheri Smith, Jack Ridl, Gloria Klinger, Angela Gary Scripps, Marilyn Schmidt and Carmen Hannah—you know how to do it without squeezing too tightly.

Thank you Sara Leeland, for liking what I put on these pages.

About the Author

Audrianne Hill taught English at Grand Haven Area Public Schools and lives in Holland along the shores of Lake Michigan. She currently sells books.

Made in the USA
Charleston, SC
07 December 2013